Blankets, Hats, and Booties

Martingale®
& C O M P A N Y

Blankets, Hats, and Booties:
To Knit and Crochet
© 2006 by Kristin Spurkland

Martingale & Company
20205 144th Avenue NE
Woodinville, WA 98072-8478 USA
www.martingale-pub.com

Printed in China
11 10 09 08 07 06   8 7 6 5 4 3 2 1

Library of Congress Cataloging-in-Publication Data
Spurkland, Kristin.
    Blankets, hats, and booties : to knit and crochet /
Kristin Spurkland.
        p. cm.
    ISBN 1-56477-652-2
1. Knitting—Patterns. 2. Crocheting—Patterns.
3. Infants' supplies. I. Title.
    TT825.S7132 2006
    746.43'2041—dc22
                                    2005028416

Mission Statement

Dedicated to providing quality products and service to inspire creativity.

Credits

President: Nancy J. Martin
CEO: Daniel J. Martin
VP and General Manager: Tom Wierzbicki
Publisher: Jane Hamada
Editorial Director: Mary V. Green
Managing Editor: Tina Cook
Technical Editor: Ann E. Smith
Copy Editor: Ellen Balstad
Design Director: Stan Green
Illustrator: Robin Strobel
Cover and Text Designer: Regina Girard
Photographer: Brent Kane

Dedication

To my father, Tobben Spurkland, and to my Norwegian ancestors, from whom I must have inherited the knitting gene.

Acknowledgments

I'd like to thank all the talented needleworkers who helped in the production of this book: Sandy Bingham, Lynn Gates, Jamie Guinn, Mary Scott Huff, and Jesse Stenberg. Special thanks to Judy Taylor, who worked the kinks out of the Cable and Lace blanket with patience, persistence, and impressive speed, and made it beautiful.

Contents

Introduction

I like making baby blankets. Because they're usually just simple squares or rectangles, I can forget about shaping and just focus on color and patterning. Finishing is often nothing more than weaving in yarn ends, some gentle blocking, and perhaps adding some embroidery or a lining.

Baby hats and booties may be more complex in shaping than blankets, but because they're small and (usually) quick to complete, I hardly notice the extra bit of focus required. And as I have told many a student struggling with the perceived imperfections of their finished baby projects, everything looks good on a baby, and who would be so mean as to critique a baby's handmade clothes?

There are a few words I'd like to share about the knit and crochet patterns in *Blankets, Hats, and Booties*. Babies arrive in a tremendous range of sizes, so the size designations such as Newborn or 0–6 Months are averages. They may or may not apply to the particular baby for whom you are knitting or crocheting. When in doubt, I err on the side of making the hat or booties a little big because babies grow fast and the item will fit them eventually.

Most of the booties in *Blankets, Hats, and Booties* are knit on double-pointed needles ranging from size 3 (3.25 mm) to 5 (3.75 mm), or crocheted on size G-6 (4 mm) to size H-8 (5 mm) hooks. In teaching bootie and sock classes, I have found that many people experience significant gauge changes when working on a small-scale project like a bootie. Experiment to find what needle size works best for you to get the size you want.

You'll notice that the patterns refer to booties and socks, and hats and caps, and you may wonder what the difference is between the various styles. Booties just cover the foot, while socks have longer cuffs that come up over the ankle. Hats come down over the crown of the head and reach the ears or cover them, while caps are shaped from the back of the head and come forward to frame the face.

The bootie and sock patterns in this book are written for one size only and should fit the average newborn. If you want a larger bootie, it's usually sufficient to go up one hook or needle size. For a smaller bootie (perhaps for a preemie—they need booties too!) go down one size.

Several blankets in *Blankets, Hats, and Booties* can easily be made larger, even afghan size. To enlarge the Granny Squares crocheted blanket, keep making squares until you have as many as you need to get the size you want. The Pinwheel crocheted blanket and Rose Leaf knitted blanket, both worked from the center out, can be increased indefinitely to any size. And the No Gauge blanket allows you to use almost any yarn to make a blanket of any size you wish, from a tiny blanket for a preemie to a bedspread, should you be so inclined. Just remember that significantly increasing the size of the blanket will require the purchase of significantly more yarn.

When making baby items to give as gifts, it's a good idea to find out the parents' preferences regarding fiber content and care requirements. Some parents prefer natural fibers and don't mind hand washing from time to time. Other parents need to be able to throw the blanket in the washer and forget about it. You want your gift to be used and appreciated, so be thoughtful when choosing yarn.

Knitting Techniques

This section outlines knitting techniques used in this book, some of which may be new to you. If you need help with more basic techniques, consult one of the many fine knitting references available. My book *Knits from the Heart* (Martingale & Company, 2004) includes more extensive how-to information.

Cable Cast On

I use the cable cast on when I need to cast on in the middle of a project. To start, you need 2 stitches on your left-hand needle. If you are casting on from scratch, this would be your slipknot plus one more cast-on stitch (use whatever cast-on method you usually employ to add the second stitch). If you are casting on within the body of a project, this would be the first 2 stitches on the left-hand needle. *Insert your right needle between the first 2 stitches on the left needle, wrap the yarn as if to knit, and pull the new stitch through. Place this new stitch on the left needle. Repeat from * until you cast on the required number of stitches.

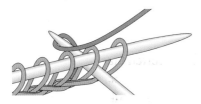

Insert needle between two stitches. Knit a stitch.

Place new stitch on left needle.

Yarn Over (YO)

Yarn overs are used in lace knitting to make the holes that create lace fabric. How a yarn over is made varies with the placement of the yarn over in the stitch pattern.

Between 2 knit stitches: Bring the yarn forward between the 2 needles, and then back over the right needle. Knit the next stitch as usual.

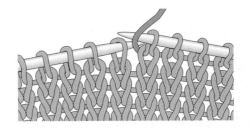

Between 2 purl stitches: Take the yarn back over the right needle, and then forward between the 2 needles. Purl the next stitch as usual.

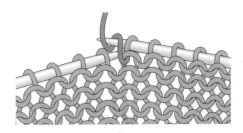

Between a knit and a purl: Bring the yarn forward, back over right needle, and then forward again. Purl the next stitch as usual.

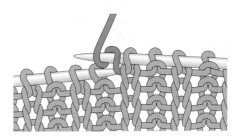

Between a purl and a knit: Take the yarn back over the right needle and knit the next stitch as usual.

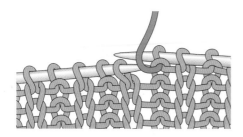

Two-Color Knitting

The easiest technique for those who are new to 2-color knitting is what is called the "pick up and drop" method. Simply knit color A for however many stitches the pattern indicates, let go of it, pick up color B from under color A, knit as indicated in the pattern, drop color B, and pick up the next color from under the previous color. Continue "picking and dropping" as necessary.

It's important to leave the "floats" (the strands of the color not in use that travel along the inside of your knitting) long enough. If the floats are too short, your knitting will pucker. Gently stretching your knitting down the right-hand needle before changing to a new color greatly reduces the chances of puckering, because it ensures that the floats will be long enough to span the distance they must cover.

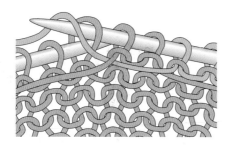

Decreases

The following decrease techniques are used in this book.

Purl Two Together through Back Loop (P2tog tbl)

Insert the right needle into the back of the next 2 stitches from left to right, wrap yarn as if to purl, pull the new stitch through, and drop the 2 worked stitches off the left needle.

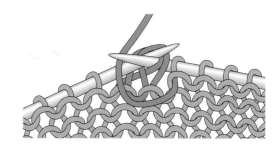

Slip, Slip, Knit (SSK)

Slip the next 2 stitches knitwise one at a time, and then insert the left needle into the fronts of the slipped stitches and knit the slipped stitches together.

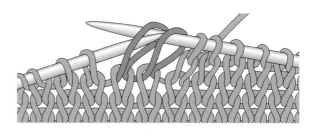

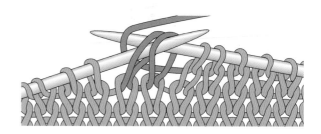

Double Decreases

There are 3 double decreases used in this book. Each one varies subtly from the others—these variations give each decrease a slightly different look. It's important to use the decrease specified in your pattern because using a different decrease will change the look of your fabric.

Sl2tog kw, K1, p2sso: Slip the next 2 stitches together knitwise, knit the next stitch, and pass the 2 slipped stitches over the knit stitch and off the needle.

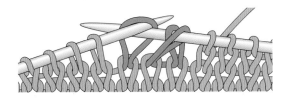

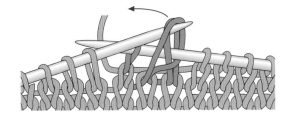

Sl2 kw 1 at a time, K1, p2sso: Slip the next 2 stitches knitwise 1 at a time, knit the next stitch, pass the 2 slipped stitches over the knit stitch and off the needle.

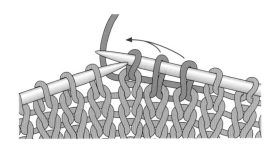

Sl1 kw, K2tog, psso: Slip the next stitch knitwise, knit the next 2 stitches together, and pass the slipped stitch over the knit-2-together stitch.

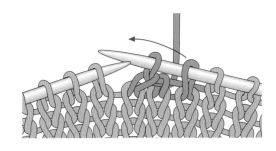

Increases

Knitting into the front and back of a stitch (K1f&b), also known as a bar increase, is the method I use the most. Knit the next stitch as usual, but leave it on the left needle. Pivot the right needle around to the back of the same stitch, and knit into the back of it. You've made 2 stitches out of 1 stitch.

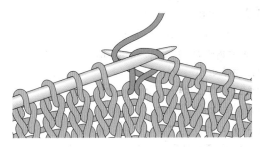

Knit into the front of the next stitch.

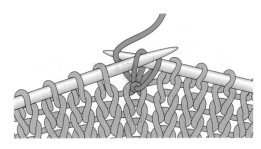

Knit into the back of the same stitch.

Sometimes you need to do a double increase. You must knit into the front, the back, and the front of the stitch. This results in 3 stitches made out of 1 stitch.

Finishing and Embellishing

Once you knit your project, make it spectacular with these finishing and decorative techniques. Simple to learn and easy to execute, they add a personal touch to your project.

Three-Needle Bind Off

I used the 3-needle bind off technique to join the ruffles on the Dots and Ruffles blanket. It's more typically used to join shoulder seams, and it is a very useful technique to know.

Place the 2 pieces to be joined on 2 different needles. Hold the pieces in your left hand, parallel, with right sides together. Insert a third needle of the same size into the first stitch on the front needle, then into the first stitch on the back needle, and knit these 2 stitches together. *Knit the next 2 stitches together (2 stitches on the right-hand needle), pass the first stitch on the right-hand needle over the second stitch and off the needle, and repeat from * until all the stitches are bound off.

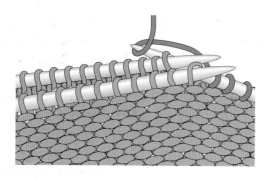

Beaded Bind Off

Beaded bind off is worked much as regular bind off (regular bind off: knit 2 stitches, *pass the first stitch worked over the second and off the needle, knit the next stitch, and repeat from *) but with a couple of extra steps. It can be worked from either the right side or the wrong side of the work. For the projects in this book, I have worked it from the wrong side.

While the instructions that follow may look complex, the technique is really not much more difficult than your usual bind off. Once you do a few stitches, you'll get the hang of it. Practice on a swatch and you'll have it down in no time. Because of the increases worked as part of the bind off, I find it best to use a needle 2 sizes smaller than that used for the main part of the project. Using the same-size needle may cause the edge to flare.

In order to do this bind off, you will need to know how to do a double increase. See "Increases" on page 7. For the beaded bind off, double increase in the first stitch, pass the first 2 increase stitches together over the third stitch and off the needle, *knit 1 stitch, pass the remaining stitch over the knit 1 stitch and off the needle, double increase, pass the middle 2 stitches together over the third stitch and off the needle, pass the first stitch over and off the needle, and repeat from * until all the stitches have been bound off.

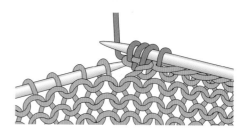

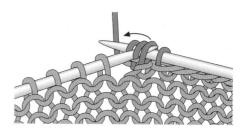

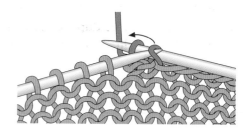

It's not crucial that you end the bind off with either a knit 1 or the double increase—depending on how many stitches you are working over you may end on either step. I usually prefer the look of starting and ending with the double increase, but it's not mandatory.

I-cord

I-cord is used to finish the Quack! hat (see page 39), and it can also be used to make ties for the hats and bonnets should you prefer not to use ribbon. Cast on the desired number of stitches onto a double-pointed needle. *Knit the stitches. Then, without turning your work, slide the stitches back to the right end of the needle. Repeat from * until the I-cord is the desired length. Bind off the stitches.

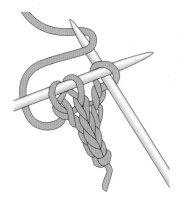

Duplicate Stitch

This technique is used to add color and detail to a finished piece of knitting. The duplicate stitch does exactly what its name implies—it duplicates an existing stitch but in a different color.

To do horizontal duplicate stitching, *bring a threaded tapestry needle from the wrong side of the work out to the right side, with the needle emerging at the base of the stitch you want to duplicate. Then insert the needle under the base of the knit stitch directly above the stitch to be duplicated. Reinsert the needle at the base of the duplicated stitch (the same place it emerged initially). Repeat from * until all the stitches to be duplicated have been worked.

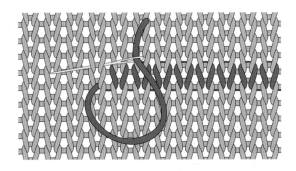

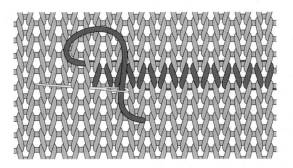

To do vertical duplicate stitching, bring a threaded tapestry needle from the wrong side of the work out to the right side at the base of the first stitch to be covered. Insert the needle from right to left through the top of the same stitch. Bring the needle down and insert it at the base of the same stitch, bringing it out again at the base of the stitch that lies directly above the one you just covered. Continue in this manner until all the stitches to be duplicated have been worked.

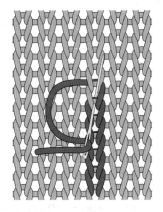

In this section you'll find instructions for crochet techniques used in this book. If you need help with basic techniques, consult your favorite crochet reference book. Also, my book *Crochet from the Heart* (Martingale & Company, 2005) includes more extensive how-to information.

Changing Color and Adding New Skeins of Yarn

The same technique is used both for changing colors and for adding a new skein of yarn when the old one runs out.

Work the last stitch of the old yarn to the final yarn over, drop the old yarn, and work the final yarn over and complete the stitch with the new yarn. Make sure to leave sufficiently long tails of each color to be able to weave them in easily.

Note that when changing colors, the change actually happens on the last yarn over of the stitch before the color change. If a pattern tells you to work 3 stitches with color A, and then 3 stitches with color B, you actually change colors on the last yarn over of the last stitch in color A. This leaves you in position to work the next stitch with color B.

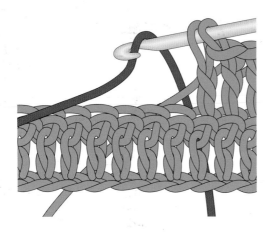

Joining Yarn on Finished Edge

Sometimes you have to add yarn to a finished edge, meaning that there is no "live" stitch to work into. One option is to make a slipknot on your hook with the new yarn, insert your hook under the first stitch to be worked, and then proceed as instructed in your pattern. I don't care for this technique, because it leaves a slipknot in my work that I have to hide. I prefer to simply insert my hook under the stitch *before* the first stitch to be worked, catch the new yarn with the hook, and draw a loop through the stitch. This anchors the new yarn to the fabric and places it in position to work the first stitch, without the use of any knots.

The initial step of inserting the hook under a stitch, hooking the yarn, and drawing it through does not count as a stitch. It's a set-up step that anchors the yarn. The first stitch is the stitch following this set-up step. You may find it helpful to mark the set-up stitch or the first stitch made after adding the new yarn, thus avoiding confusion when you come back to the place where you joined the yarn on the subsequent row or round.

Yarn Substitution and Hook Size

When crocheting, I frequently use a hook size larger than that recommended on the yarn label, because I prefer the looser, more drapey fabric I get as a result. Therefore, if you are going to substitute any of the yarns used in this book, match the weight of the yarn, not the hook size on the yarn label. If I used a DK-weight yarn and an I-9 (5.5 mm) hook, look for another DK-weight yarn, not a yarn that recommends an I-9 hook.

Finishing

The first step in creating a beautiful gift is crocheting it up. Expert finishing is the second. Below are two of my favorite techniques for easy, flawless finishing.

Overcast Seam

There are a number of ways to sew your crochet pieces together. My recommendation is that you use whatever technique works best for you, even if it's something you make up yourself. The overcast seam is the one I use the most.

To make an overcast seam, lay the pieces to be seamed side by side, right sides up. With project yarn threaded through a tapestry needle, *insert the needle under the back loop of the edge stitch from each piece, pull yarn through, and repeat from * to the end of the seam.

Duplicate Stitch Join

This technique, based on the duplicate stitch used in knitting, was created because I didn't like the look of the usual method of finishing in-the-round projects (joining the last stitch of the round to the first stitch of the round with a slip stitch).

After working the final stitch of your project, break the yarn and fasten off. (Omit the step of joining the last stitch of the round to the first stitch of the round with a slip stitch if your pattern instructs you to do this.)

Thread the tail though a tapestry needle. Insert the needle from front to back under the legs of the second stitch of the round, and then from front to back under the back leg of the last stitch of the round. You are covering (duplicating) the first stitch of the round. Weave the tail in on the wrong side of the work.

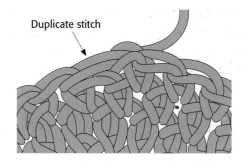

Duplicate stitch

Embellishing, Lining, and Blocking

Embellishments such as French knots and linings can take your projects from ordinary to extraordinary. And careful blocking improves the look of any project.

Making French Knots

Thread yarn through a tapestry needle and bring the needle up through the fabric from the wrong side. Holding the yarn taut with your left hand, wrap the yarn around the needle twice (wrap more times for a larger knot). Maintaining the tension on the yarn, reinsert the tapestry needle through the fabric near the place where it originally emerged. Pull the yarn and needle through, making sure to hold the yarn taut throughout. I like to knot the yarn ends on the inside of the fabric when making French knots, to avoid the possibility of them being pulled out.

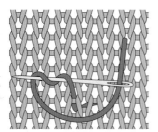

Wrap yarn around needle
2 or more times.

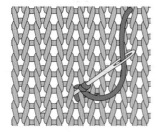

Insert yarn close to
emerging point.

Lining a Blanket

Some of the patterns in *Blankets, Hats, and Booties* specify that a lining be added. But you can line any blanket, even if it doesn't obviously require a lining. Linings have many benefits. They hide decidedly "wrong" sides of your knitted or crocheted fabric, they make the blanket warmer, and they add a fun design element. They also keep little fingers and toes from poking through the fabric or pulling stitches if this is a concern.

Lining is simple to do. It just requires a little time and patience. Always preshrink the fabric you're using to line the blanket; then cut the fabric to the size indicated in the pattern. If you have a serger, serge the edges. If you don't have a serger, don't worry about it; serging makes the job a little easier but isn't a necessity. Fold the fabric edges, serged or not, under ½" all the way around. Pin the wrong side of the fabric to the wrong side of the blanket and hand stitch it into place, using a sewing needle and thread.

Blocking

Blocking opens up lace patterns, relaxes cables, evens out any irregularities of tension, and shapes fabric. It's the final step to making your needlework look fabulous.

To wet block, wash the item just as you would normally, and then lay it out flat on towels and gently coax it into shape. Gentle is the operative word here; you never want to pull roughly on your needlework. Grab a tape measure and your pattern instructions, and shape the piece to the dimensions given in the pattern. Then wait patiently for it to dry. If you remove your work when it is still damp, it may very well revert to its original, pre-blocked shape.

Lace, cables, and stranded (2-color patterned) projects usually require wet blocking to achieve their correct dimensions. However, for many projects steam blocking is quite sufficient. To steam block, place your project on a covered surface (an ironing board for a small item, a table covered with a towel for larger items), turn your iron to a steam setting, and have your tape measure and pattern within reach. Hold the steam iron an inch or so over your project—direct contact may melt, scorch, or otherwise damage it!—and let the steam permeate the fabric. Shape your project to the size given in the pattern, and then wait until it is completely cool and dry before moving it.

Note that steaming may not be appropriate for acrylic and other man-made fibers, as some of them may scorch. If you're unsure, use your swatch as a test piece before steaming your project.

Abbreviations

alt	alternate
beg	begin(ning)
blo	back loop only
BO	bind off
ch(s)	chain(s)
ch sp	chain space
cn	cable needle
CO	cast on
cont	continue
dc	double crochet
dc2tog	double crochet 2 stitches together
dec	decrease(ing)
dpn(s)	double-pointed needle(s)
g	gram(s)
inc	increase(ing)
K	knit
K1 tbl	knit 1 through the back loop
K1f&b	knit into front and back of stitch (see page 7)
K2tog	knit 2 stitches together
K3tog	knit 3 stitches together
kw	knitwise
m	meter(s)
MC	main color
mm	millimeter(s)
P	purl
p2sso	pass 2 slipped stitches over
P2tog	purl 2 stitches together
P2tog tbl	purl 2 stitches together through the back loops
P3tog	purl 3 stitches together
patt	pattern
PM	place marker
psso	pass slipped stitch over
PU	pick up and knit
pw	purlwise
rem	remain(ing)
rep(s)	repeat(s)
rnd(s)	round(s)
RS	right side(s)
sc	single crochet
sc2tog	single crochet 2 stitches together
sc3tog	single crochet 3 stitches together
sk	skip
sl	slip
sl1 kw, K2tog, psso	slip 1 stitch knitwise, knit 2 stitches together, pass the slipped stitch over the knit-2-together stitch
sl2 kw 1 at a time, K1, p2sso	slip 2 stitches knitwise 1 at a time, knit 1 stitch, pass the slipped stitches over the knit stitch
sl2tog kw	slip 2 stitches together knitwise
sl2tog kw, K1, p2sso	slip 2 stitches knitwise, knit 1 stitch, pass the slipped stitches over the knit stitch
sp(s)	space(s)
SSK	slip, slip, knit (see page 6)
st(s)	stitch(es)
St st	stockinette stitch
tbl	through back loop(s)
tch	turning chain
tog	together
WS	wrong side(s)
wyib	with yarn in back
wyif	with yarn in front
yd(s)	yard(s)
YO	yarn over

Yarn Weights

Yarn-Weight Symbol and Category Names	1 Super Fine	2 Fine	3 Light	4 Medium	5 Bulky	6 Super Bulky
Types of Yarns in Category	Sock, Fingering, Baby	Sport, Baby	DK, Light Worsted	Worsted, Afghan, Aran	Chunky, Craft, Rug	Bulky, Roving

Yarn Conversions

Yards x .91 = meters

Meters x 1.09 = yards

Grams x .0352 = ounces

Ounces x 28.35 = grams

Adjusting Hat Sizes

Follow these steps to adjust sizes for knit and crochet hats worked from the top down.

1. Find your desired finished circumference.
2. Find the corresponding diameter.
3. Starting your hat from the top, work increases as given in the pattern until the hat measures approximately the diameter shown for the circumference you want.
4. Once you've reached your desired diameter, work even without increasing until the hat is the depth you want, making allowances for any borders you may want to add.

This formula works best for hats knit in stockinette stitch or crocheted in single crochet. More complicated stitch patterns will require a bit more calculating and experimenting on your part to ensure a proper fit.

Diameter	Approx. Circumference
1½"	4¾"
1¾"	5½"
2"	6¼"
2¼"	7"
2½"	7¾"
2¾"	8½"
3"	9½"
3¼"	10¼"
3½"	11"
3¾"	11¾"
4"	12½"

Diameter	Approx. Circumference
4¼"	13¼"
4½"	14"
4¾"	15"
5"	16"
5½"	17"
5¾"	18"
6"	19"
6¼"	20"
6¾"	21"
7"	22"

Calculating Hat Circumference

If you want to make a hat in a circumference that isn't in the list, divide the desired circumference by 3.1416 to obtain the diameter you need to knit to. For example, if you need to make a hat with a 5" circumference, divide 5" by 3.1416, which equals 1.59". While 1.59" is a little difficult to measure, you know that the diameter needs to be a bit larger than 1½" and a bit less than 1¾".

Stripes

Irregular stripes add color and pattern to this simple stockinette stitch blanket. Neutral colors make it suitable for both boys and girls—a good idea if you don't know the gender of the impending new arrival. The color-blocked socks can be made in identical pairs, but I like the idea of making each half of the pair different, allowing you to use all the colors of the blanket. And an easy stockinette stitch hat with a seed stitch border completes the set.

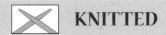

KNITTED

Finished Sizes

Blanket: 28½" x 32"

Hat: Newborn (6 Months, 1 Year)
   14½ (16, 17½)" circumference

Socks: 0–6 Months

Blanket Materials

⧫ Cotton Cashmere from Debbie Bliss (85% cotton, 15% cashmere; 50 g; 95 m) in the following colors :

A	2 skeins	16 Sage
B	2 skeins	7 Pink
C	2 skeins	3 Cream
D	2 skeins	4 Grey
E	2 skeins	9 Grape
F	2 skeins	14 Blue

⧫ 24" circular needle in size 3 (3.25 mm)

⧫ 24" circular needle in size 5 (3.75 mm), or size required to obtain gauge

⧫ Tapestry needle

Hat and Socks Materials

⧫ Cotton Cashmere from Debbie Bliss (85% cotton, 15% cashmere; 50 g; 95 m) in the following colors :

A	1 skein	16 Sage

Leftover yarns B–F from blanket *or* 1 new skein of each (will make multiple hats and socks)

⧫ Stitch markers

⧫ Tapestry needle

⧫ **For hat:** 16" circular needle in size 3 (3.25 mm), 16" circular needle in size 5 (3.75 mm), and size 5 (3.75 mm) double-pointed needles

⧫ **For socks:** Size 4 (3.5 mm) double-pointed needles, stitch holder or waste yarn

Gauge

22 sts and 28 rows = 4" in St st on size 5 needle

Seed Stitch

All rows: *K1, P1, rep from *, end K1.

Stripe Sequence

(Worked in St st)

4 rows B

8 rows C

2 rows D

4 rows E

6 rows F *

2 rows A**

6 rows B

4 rows C

8 rows D

2 rows E

4 rows F

6 rows A

2 rows B

6 rows C

4 rows D

8 rows E

2 rows F

4 rows A

6 rows B

2 rows C

6 rows D

4 rows E

8 rows F

2 rows A

4 rows B

6 rows C

2 rows D

6 rows E

4 rows F

8 rows A

2 rows B

4 rows C

6 rows D

2 rows E

(continued on page 18)

6 rows F

4 rows A

8 rows B

2 rows C

4 rows D

6 rows E

2 rows F

6 rows A

Don't carry yarns up the side of the work; instead, break yarn at the end of each stripe.

Blanket Instructions

With A and size 3 needle, CO 149 sts. Work in seed st for 5 rows.

Change to size 5 needle and B, work stripe sequence in St st, starting with a knit (RS) row. Work through entire stripe sequence 1 time, then through * once more (6 rows F completed).

Top Border

Knit 1 row with A.

Change to size 3 needle and work 4 rows seed st.

Next row: BO in seed st.

Side Borders

Using A and size 3 needle, PU 169 sts along side edge. Work seed st for 4 rows. BO in seed st on 5th row.

Rep along 2nd side edge. Weave in ends.

Hat Instructions

With A and 16" circular needle in size 3, CO 80 (88, 96) sts. Join into a circle, being careful not to twist sts, and PM for beg of rnd.

Work in seed st for 5 rnds as follows:

Rnds 1, 3, and 5: *K1, P1, rep from * around.

Rnds 2 and 4: *P1, K1, rep from * around.

Change to 16" circular needle in size 5 and B, and work stripe sequence as for blanket through ** (2 rnds A completed).

Shape Crown

Continuing stripe sequence as for blanket, work crown as follows:

Next rnd: Knit.

Next rnd: *K8 (9, 10), K2tog, rep from * around.

Rep last 2 rnds as established, working 1 less st before the dec with each dec rnd and changing to size 5 dpns when necessary, until you've completed the *K5 (3, 3), K2tog* rnd. From this point forward, omit plain rnd between dec rnds. Cont to dec every rnd until you've completed the *K2tog* rnd. 8 sts rem. Break yarn, thread through tapestry needle, and draw through rem sts.

Socks Instructions

With A and size 4 dpns, CO 22 sts. Divide sts over 3 dpns, join in the rnd, and PM.

Work K1, P1 ribbing for 2".

Knit 1 rnd. Break A.

Heel

Join C at beg of rnd. K10, turn and purl across same 10 sts—these are heel sts. Place rem 12 sts on holder or waste yarn.

Next row: Knit.

Next row: Purl.

Rep these 2 rows 2 more times.

Turn Heel

Row 1: K5, K2tog, K1.

Row 2: P2, P2tog tbl, P1.

Row 3: K3, K2tog, K1.

Row 4: P4, P2tog tbl, P1—6 sts. Break C.

Gusset

Sl first 3 heel sts onto dpn. PM to mark beg of rnd and join B. K3, PU 5 sts along selvage of heel flap, PM (this will be a "gusset marker"), K2, SSK, K4, K2tog, K2 from holder, PM (another "gusset marker"), PU 5 sts along other heel flap selvage, knit last 3 heel sts—26 sts.

Shape Gusset

Next rnd: Knit to 2 sts before first gusset marker, K2tog, knit to next gusset marker, SSK, knit to end of rnd—24 sts.

Next rnd: Knit.

Rep last 2 rnds until 20 sts rem.

Knit 10 rnds. Break B at end of rnd 10.

Shape Toe

Join D.

Next rnd: Knit.

Next rnd: K3, K2tog, SSK, K6, K2tog, SSK, K3—16 sts.

Next rnd: Knit.

Next rnd: K2, K2tog, SSK, K4, K2tog, SSK, K2—12 sts.

Break yarn, thread through tapestry needle, and draw through rem sts. Weave in ends.

Make second sock using colors E, B, C, and F.

Cables and Lace

Loose cables and lacy leaves make this an elegant design for Baby and a great project for knitters looking for a bit of a challenge.

KNITTED

Finished Sizes

Blanket: 26½" x 30"

Cap: 0–6 Months (cap can be blocked to accommodate larger sizes)

Socks: 0–6 Months

Blanket Materials

- 8 skeins of Baby Cashmerino from Debbie Bliss (55% merino wool, 33% microfiber, 12% cashmere; 50 g; 125 m), color 503 Fern
- 24" circular needle in size 3 (3.25 mm)
- Cable needle
- Stitch markers (optional)

Cap and Socks Materials

- 2 skeins of Baby Cashmerino from Debbie Bliss (55% merino wool, 33% microfiber, 12% cashmere; 50 g; 125 m), color 503 Fern
- Tapestry needle
- **For cap:** 16" (or longer) size 3 (3.25 mm) circular needle or size 3 (3.25 mm) straight needles, 1 yd ½"-wide ribbon, sewing needle, matching thread
- **For socks:** Size 3 (3.25 mm) double-pointed needles, cable needle, stitch holder or waste yarn, stitch markers

Gauge

31 sts and 35 rows = 4" over cable chart and lace chart (lightly blocked)

Seed Stitch

Row 1: *K1, P1, rep from * across row.

Row 2: *P1, K1, rep from * across row.

Rep these 2 rows for patt.

Blanket Instructions

Lower Border

With 24" circular needle in size 3, CO 206 sts. Work in seed st for 8 rows.

Next row: (K1, P1) twice, K1, purl to last 5 sts, (P1, K1) twice, P1.

Begin Chart

Keeping first 5 sts and last 5 sts in seed st as established, beg working charts across center 196 sts as follows: Work across (cable chart, lace chart) 3 times, then work across cable chart once more, noting that there is a St st before, after, and between each of the 3 cables.

Using Charts

To stay on track when following the charts, place a marker at the start of each chart repeat.

Cont as established until you've worked through the cable chart 10 times total (lace chart 20 times total). Work rows 1–4 of each chart once more.

Top Border

Work 8 rows in seed st.

Next row: BO in seed st.

Finishing

Block blanket. Wet blocking (see page 12) will give you the best results. Weave in ends.

Cap Instructions

With size 3 circular needle, CO 86 sts. Do not join. Work in seed st for 6 rows.

Next row: Purl.

Next row: K1, work across (cable chart, lace chart) once, then work across cable chart 1 more time, K1.

Next row: P1, work across charts as established, P1.

Cont in this manner, keeping the first st and the last st in St st until you've worked through rows 1–12 of lace chart 3 times (1½ reps of cable chart completed).

Next row: BO first 28 sts, cont lace chart as established across center 30 sts, BO rem 28 sts. Break yarn.

Rejoin yarn for a WS row, P1, cont lace chart as established, P1.

Cable chart
28 sts

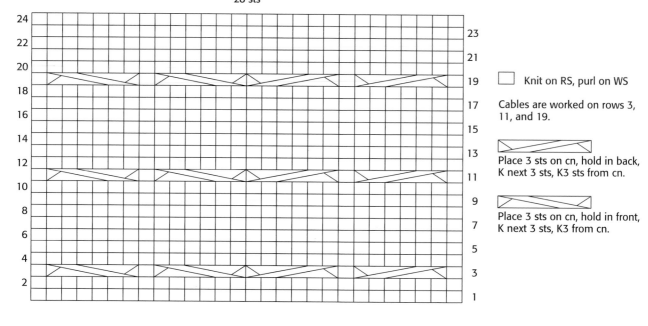

Knit on RS, purl on WS

Cables are worked on rows 3, 11, and 19.

Place 3 sts on cn, hold in back, K next 3 sts, K3 sts from cn.

Place 3 sts on cn, hold in front, K next 3 sts, K3 from cn.

Lace chart
28 sts

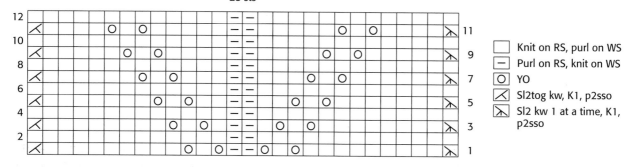

Knit on RS, purl on WS

Purl on RS, knit on WS

YO

Sl2tog kw, K1, p2sso

Sl2 kw 1 at a time, K1, p2sso

Next row: K1, cont lace chart as established, K1.

Cont in this manner until you've completed 5 reps of the lace chart from the CO edge. BO sts.

Finishing

Sew back seams of cap.

Lower border: PU 90 sts along lower edge of cap. Work 5 rows seed st.

Next row: BO in seed st.

Weave in ends. Block cap gently; over blocking will make cap too big.

Make ties: Cut ribbon into two 18" lengths and sew to lower front corners of cap.

Socks Instructions

With size 3 dpns, CO 24 sts. Divide sts over 3 dpns, join into rnd and PM.

Work K1, P1 ribbing for 4 rnds.

Work cables as follows:

Rnds 1 and 2: Knit.

Rnd 3: *K1, sl next 3 sts to cn and hold in back, K3, K3 from cn, K1, rep from * around.

Rnds 4–8: Knit.

Rep rnds 1–8 one more time, and then rnds 1–6 one more time.

Heel

K10, turn and purl across same 10 sts—these are heel
   sts. Place rem 14 sts on holder.

Next row: Knit.

Next row: Purl.

Rep these 2 rows 2 more times.

Turn Heel

Row 1: K5, K2tog, K1.

Row 2: P2, P2tog tbl, P1.

Row 3: K3, K2tog, K1.

Row 4: P4, P2tog tbl, P1—6 sts.

Gusset

K3, PM to mark beg of rnd, K3, PU 5 sts along
   selvage of heel flap, PM (this will be a "gusset
   marker"), K2, SSK, K6, K2tog, K2 from holder,
   PM (another "gusset marker"), PU 5 sts along
   other heel flap selvage, knit last 3 heel sts—
   28 sts.

Shape Gusset

Next rnd: Knit to 2 sts before first gusset marker,
   K2tog, knit to next gusset marker, SSK, knit to
   end of rnd.

Next rnd: Knit.

Rep last 2 rnds until 22 sts rem.

Knit 10 rnds.

Shape Toe

Next rnd: K3, K2tog, SSK, K8, K2tog, SSK, K3—
   18 sts.

Next rnd: Knit.

Next rnd: K2, K2tog, SSK, K6, K2tog, SSK, K2—
   14 sts.

Break yarn, thread through tapestry needle, and
   draw through rem sts. Weave in ends.

Filet Crochet

A traditional crochet form is made current with the addition of French knot details. The accompanying cap and booties are simple and fast to make, with ribbon and French knot embellishments.

CROCHETED

Finished Sizes

Blanket: 29" x 30"

Cap: Newborn (6–18 Months)

Booties: 0–6 Months

Blanket Materials

- 6 skeins of Cotton Cashmere from Debbie Bliss (85% cotton, 15% cashmere; 50 g; 95 m), color 13 Teal ⟨3⟩
- Small amounts of Cotton Cashmere from Debbie Bliss (85% cotton, 15% cashmere; 50 g; 95 m), in contrasting colors for French knots; colors shown: 5 Orange, 16 Sage, 9 Grape ⟨3⟩
- Size H-8 (5 mm) crochet hook
- Tapestry needle

Cap and Booties Materials

- 1 skein of Cotton Cashmere from Debbie Bliss (85% cotton, 15% cashmere; 50 g; 95 m), color 13 Teal (will make both the cap and booties) ⟨3⟩
- Small amounts of Cotton Cashmere from Debbie Bliss (85% cotton, 15% cashmere; 50 g; 95 m), in contrasting colors for French knots; colors shown: 5 Orange, 16 Sage, 9 Grape ⟨3⟩
- Size H-8 (5 mm) crochet hook
- **For cap:** 2 yards of ⅝"-wide ribbon

Gauge

16.25 sts and 7.25 rows = 4" in filet crochet patt

Blanket Instructions

With Teal, ch 120 sts, turn. Sk first ch, sc 119, turn.

Filet crochet set-up row (counts as row 1 first time through): Ch 3, sk first sc, dc in next 8 sts, *ch 2, sk 2 sts, dc in next st, ch 2, sk 2 sts, dc in next 7 sts, rep from * across, end dc in each of last 2 sts, turn. Go to row 2 of filet crochet patt.

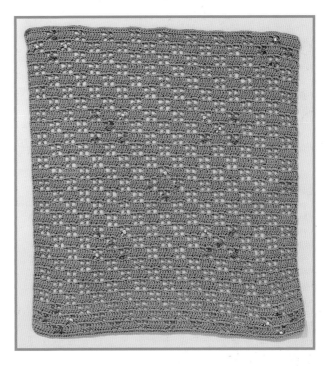

Filet Crochet Pattern

Note that each ch-2 sp counts as 2 sts.

Rows 1 and 2: Ch 3, sk first dc, dc in next 8 dc, *ch 2, sk 2 sts, dc in next st, ch 2, sk 2 sts, dc in next 7 sts, rep from * across row, end dc in last st, dc in top of tch. Turn.

Rows 3 and 4: Ch 3, sk first st, dc in next 2 sts, *ch 2, sk 2 sts, dc in next st, ch 2, sk 2 sts, dc in next 7 sts, rep from * across row, end ch 2, sk 2 sts, dc in next st, ch 2, sk 2 sts, dc in last 2 sts, dc in top of tch, turn.

Rep these 4 rows for patt.

NOTE: When working double crochet stitches across the 2 chain stitches along the top of the open spaces, you have 2 options. You can work directly into the chain stitches, or you can work into the chain space. Working into the chain space is faster and easier, but some prefer the look of working into the chain itself. Work however you like, but make sure to work 2 double crochet stitches for each open square.

Cont in filet crochet patt until you've completed rows 1–4 thirteen times. Work rows 1 and 2 one more time.

Next 2 rows: Ch 1, sc across. Break yarn and fasten off. Weave in ends.

Using your 3 contrasting colors, and double-stranding the yarn, make French knots (see page 12) in the centers of some of the open spaces as shown, placing colors randomly. Rather than weaving in the ends of the French knot yarn, I like to tie them off and clip them to about ¼" long. The ends are going to show no matter what, and tied off this way they make an attractive design element on the wrong side. Just be sure to tie them securely so that they can't be pulled free.

Cap Instructions

Back of Cap

With Teal, ch 5 and join into ring with sl st.

Rnd 1: Ch 3, 11 dc in ring, sl st in top of beg ch—12 sts.

Rnd 2: Ch 3, 1 dc in base of ch, 2 dc in next 11 sts, sl st in top of beg ch—24 sts.

Rnd 3: Ch 3, 2 dc in next st, (dc in next st, 2 dc in next st) 11 times, sl st in top of beg chain—36 sts.

Rnd 4: Ch 3, dc in next st, 2 dc in next st, (dc in next 2 sts, 2 dc in next st) 11 times, sl st in top of beg ch—48 sts. Size Newborn, go to **.

Rnd 5: Ch 3, dc in next 2 sts, 2 dc in next st, (dc in next 3 sts, 2 dc in next st) 11 times, sl st in top of beg ch—60 sts. Size 6–18 Months, go to**.

**Top and Sides of Cap

Filet crochet set-up row (counts as row 1 first time through): Ch 3, dc2tog over next 2 sts, dc in next 13 sts, (ch 2, sk 2 sts, dc in next st, ch 2, sk 2 sts, dc in next 7 sts) once (twice), ch 2, sk 2 sts, dc in next st, ch 2, sk 2 sts, dc in next 15 sts—47 (59) sts. Turn. Go to row 2 of filet crochet patt below.

Filet Crochet Pattern

Rows 1 and 2: Ch 3, sk first st, dc in next 14 sts, (ch 2, sk 2 sts, dc in next st, ch 2, sk 2 sts, dc in next 7 sts) once (twice), ch 2, sk 2 sts, dc in next st, ch 2, sk 2 sts, dc in next 15 sts, turn.

Rows 3 and 4: Ch 3, sk first st, dc in next 8 sts, (ch 2, sk 2 sts, dc in next st, ch 2, sk 2 sts, dc in next 7 sts) 2 (3) times, dc in next 2 sts, turn.

Work rows 1–4 one time, then rows 1–2 one more time.

Next row: Ch 1, sc across row. Break yarn and fasten off. Weave in ends.

With single strands of contrast color yarns, make French knots in the center of the sps.

Cut ribbon into two 1-yd lengths and thread through lower front corners for doubled ties.

Booties Instructions

Shape Toe

With Teal, ch 2. Work 6 sc in second ch from hook, PM in first sc worked. Do not turn.

Rnd 1: 2 sc in marked st. This will join work into a circle. 2 sc in next 5 sts—12 sts.

PM in last st of rnd. Move marker to last st of each subsequent rnd.

Rnd 2: *Sc in next 5 sts, 2 sc in next st, rep from * around—14 sts.

Rnd 3: *Sc in next 6 sts, 2 sc in next st, rep from * around—16 sts.

Rnd 4: *Sc in next 7 sts, 2 sc in next st, rep from * around—18 sts.

Sc 5 rnds even.

Heel

Sc in first st, turn. Remove marker at this point.

(Ch 1, sc in next 14 sts, turn) 2 times.

Ch 1, sc in next 4 sts, (sc2tog) 3 times, sc in last 4 sts, turn—11 sts.

Ch 1, sc 11, turn.

Ch 1, sc in next 4 sts, sc3tog, sc in last 4 sts, turn—9 sts.

Ch 1, sc 9. Break yarn and fasten off.

Sew center back heel seam.

Rejoin yarn at center back heel, and sc 2 rows around foot opening. Finish the last rnd by joining the last st of rnd to the first st of rnd with a sl st or with duplicate st join (page 11). Break yarn and fasten off. Weave in ends.

Make 1 French knot in each of the 3 contrasting colors, placed along the front of the foot opening, or make many French knots placed all over the foot for a polka-dot effect. Use single strands of yarn.

Colorblock Crochet

Large, colorful squares are edged with a contrast color and then sewn together to make the blanket. The hat incorporates the first part of the square, and then finishes with rounds of back loop single crochet; back loop single crochet is also used for the simple, sweet booties.

CROCHETED

Finished Sizes

Blanket: 29" x 29"

Hat: 0–6 Months (6–18 Months)
14¼ (16)" circumference

Booties: 0–6 Months

Blanket Materials

- Cotton Patine from Elsebeth Lavold (100% cotton; 50 g; 110 m) in the following colors (3):

A	2 skeins	6 Lilac
B	1 skein	08 Sea Holly
C	1 skein	18 Linden
D	1 skein	03 Driftwood
E	1 skein	11 Willow
F	3 skeins	01 Porcelain

- Size 7 (4.5 mm) crochet hook
- Stitch marker
- Tapestry needle

Hat and Booties Materials

- Cotton Patine from Elsebeth Lavold (100% cotton; 50 g; 110 m) in the following colors (3):

  Leftover yarns A and F from blanket *or* 1 skein in each of 2 colors of your choice
- Size 7 (4.5 mm) crochet hook
- Stitch marker
- Tapestry needle

Gauge

Each completed square measures approximately 7" x 7".

18 sts and 24 rows = 4" in blo sc

Blanket Instructions

Make 16 squares—4 squares with A as the MC and 3 squares each with B, C, D, and E as the MC. Use F for rnds 8 and 9 of all squares.

Square

Ch 6. Join with sl st to form ring.

Rnd 1: Ch 3, 15 dc in ring. Join last dc to top of beg ch with sl st—16 sts.

Rnd 2: Ch 4, dc in next dc, *ch 1, dc in next dc, rep from * around, ending with ch 1, join with sl st in 3rd ch of beg ch 4.

Rnd 3: Sl st in ch-1 sp, ch 3, 2 dc in same ch-1 sp, *ch 1, 3 dc in next sp, rep from * around, ending with ch 1, join with sl st in top of beg ch—48 dc.

Rnd 4: Ch 3, dc in each of next 2 dc, *ch 1, dc in each of next 3 dc, rep from * around, ending with ch 1, join with sl st in top of beg ch—48 dc.

Rnd 5: Ch 8, dc in next ch-1 sp, *(ch 3, dc in next sp) 3 times, ch 5, dc in next sp, rep from * twice more, (ch 3, dc in next sp) 2 more times, ch 3, join with sl st in 3rd chain of beg ch 8.

Rnd 6: Sl st in ch-5 sp, ch 3, (2 dc, ch 3, 3 dc) in same sp, *(ch 1, 3 dc in next sp) 3 times, ch 1, (3 dc, ch 3, 3 dc) in next sp, rep from * twice more, (ch 1, 3 dc in next sp) 3 times, ch 1, join with sl st in top of beg ch.

Rnd 7: Sl st in next 2 dc, (sl st, ch 3, 2 dc, ch 3, 3 dc) in ch-3 corner sp, *(ch 1, dc in each of next 3 dc) 5 times, ch 1, (3 dc, ch 3, 3 dc) in next sp, rep from * twice more, (ch 1, dc in each of next 3 dc) 5 times, ch 1, join with sl st in top of beg ch. Break yarn and fasten off.

Rnd 8: With RS facing, join F in any corner sp, *(sc, ch 1, sc) in corner sp, blo sc in each dc and ch to next corner, rep from * around, join with a sl st in first sc.

Rnd 9: Blo sc in next sc, *(sc, ch 1, sc) in next ch-1 corner sp, blo sc to next corner, rep from * to end of rnd, join with sl st in first sc. Break F and fasten off. Weave in ends.

Sew squares together as follows or however you wish.

Top row: D, A, B, E

Second row: E, C, D, A

Third row: B, A, C, D

Bottom row: C, E, A, B

Border

With RS facing, join F in any corner sp. Blo sc around, working corners as for individual squares, and working 1 ch st between squares.

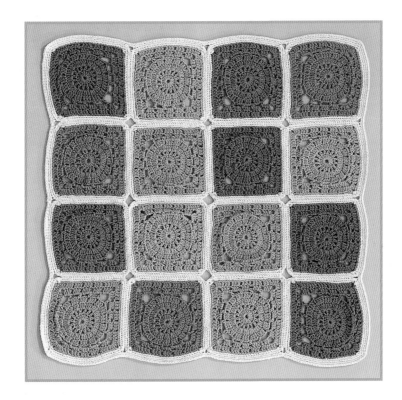

Next rnd: Blo sc around, working corners as established. Break yarn, fasten off, and weave in ends.

Hat Instructions

With A, work through rnd 4 of square—48 dc at end of rnd 4. Change to F at end of rnd.

Size 0–6 Months: Blo sc in each dc and ch around—64 sts. Blo sc in each blo sc around until hat measures 5" from start of crown. Break yarn and fasten off. Weave in ends.

Size 6–18 Months: Blo sc in each dc and ch around—64 sts.

Next rnd: *Blo sc in each of next 7 sts, 2 blo sc in next st, rep from * around—72 sts.

Next rnd: Blo sc around. Rep this rnd until hat measures 5½" from start of crown. Break yarn and fasten off. Weave in ends.

Booties Instructions

Toe

With A, ch 2. Work 6 sc in second ch from hook, PM in first sc worked. Do not turn.

Rnd 1: 2 blo sc in marked st. This will join work into a circle. 2 blo sc in next 5 sts—12 sts.

PM in last st of rnd. Move marker to last st of each subsequent rnd.

Rnd 2: *Blo sc in next 5 sts, 2 blo sc in next st, rep from * around—14 sts.

Rnd 3: *Blo sc in next 6 sts, 2 blo sc in next st, rep from * around—16 sts.

Rnd 4: *Blo sc in next 7 sts, 2 blo sc in next st, rep from * around—18 sts.

Blo sc 5 rnds even.

Heel

Sc in first st, turn. Remove marker at this point.

(Ch 1, sc in next 14 sts, turn) 2 times.

Ch 1, sc in next 4 sts, (sc2tog) 3 times, sc in last 4 sts, turn—11 sts.

Ch 1, sc 11, turn.

Ch 1, sc in next 4 sts, sc3tog, sc in last 4 sts, turn—9 sts.

Ch 1, sc 9. Break yarn and fasten off.

Sew center back heel seam.

Rejoin yarn at center back heel, and sc around foot opening. Join F and blo sc 2 rnds. Finish the last rnd by joining the last st of rnd to the first st of rnd with a sl st or with duplicate st join (page 11). Break yarn and fasten off. Weave in ends.

Diamond Brocade

A simple pattern stitch, colorful embroidery, and an unusual edge
treatment combine to create a knockout set for Baby.

KNITTED

Finished Sizes

Blanket: 30" x 32"

Hat: 0–6 Months
16½" circumference

Booties: 0–6 Months

NOTE: Because of the large pattern repeat, the hat is written for one size only. To make a smaller hat, go down one needle size. To make a larger hat, go up one needle size.

Blanket Materials

- 8 skeins of Cotton Classic from Tahki (100% cotton; 50 g; 108 yds), color 3336 Chocolate ⬛4
- Small amounts of Cotton Classic from Tahki (100% cotton; 50 g; 108 yds), in contrasting colors for embroidery; blanket as shown uses 3725 Green, 3812 Pale Blue, 3938 Pink, 3201 Oyster, 3227 Taupe ⬛4
- 24" circular needle in size 6 (4 mm)
- 24" circular needle in size 4 (3.5 mm)
- 1 additional size 4 (3.5 mm) needle for beaded bind off
- Tapestry needle
- 1 yard of preshrunk cotton fabric, at least 36" wide
- Sewing needle
- Sewing thread

Hat and Booties Materials

- 1 skein of Cotton Classic from Tahki (100% cotton; 50 g; 108 yds), color 3336 Chocolate ⬛4
- Small amounts of Cotton Classic from Tahki (100% cotton; 50 g; 108 yds), in contrasting colors for embroidery ⬛4
- Stitch markers
- Tapestry needle
- **For hat:** 16" circular needle in size 4 (3.5 mm), 16" circular needle in size 6 (4 mm), size 6 (4 mm) double-pointed needles
- **For booties:** Size 4 (3.5 mm) double-pointed needles, stitch holder or waste yarn

Gauge

22 sts and 30 rows = 4" on size 6 needle over diamond brocade

Diamond Brocade

Odd-numbered rows are RS rows.

Row 1: K10, *P1, K17, rep from * across, end P1, K10.

Rows 2 and 18: P9, *K1, P1, K1, P15, rep from * across, end K1, P1, K1, P9.

Rows 3 and 17: K8, *P1, K3, P1, K13, rep from * across, end P1, K3, P1, K8.

Rows 4 and 16: P7, *K1, P5, K1, P11, rep from * across, end K1, P5, K1, P7.

Rows 5 and 15: K6, *P1, K7, P1, K9, rep from * across, end P1, K7, P1, K6.

Rows 6 and 14: P5, *K1, P9, K1, P7, rep from * across, end K1, P9, K1, P5.

Rows 7 and 13: K4, *P1, K11, P1, K5, rep from * across, end P1, K11, P1, K4.

Rows 8 and 12: P3, *K1, P13, K1, P3, rep from * across, end K1, P13, K1, P3.

Rows 9 and 11: K2, *P1, K15, P1, K1, rep from * across, end P1, K15, P1, K2.

Row 10: P1, *K1, P17, rep from * across, end K1, P1.

Rep these 18 rows for patt.

Blanket Instructions

With Chocolate and size 6 circular needle, CO 165 sts.

Beg diamond brocade patt. Work rows 1–18 for 13 times, and then work row 1 one more time.

Change to size 4 circular needle and knit 2 rows.

Work beaded BO (see page 8).

Lower Edge

With RS facing and size 4 circular needle, PU 165 sts along opposite edge. Knit 2 rows. Work beaded BO.

Sides

With RS facing and size 4 circular needle, PU 175 sts along side edge. Knit 2 rows. Work beaded BO.

Rep on 2nd side edge.

With yarns in contrasting colors, work embroidery in center of diamonds as shown in chart.

Line blanket (see page 12).

Diamond Brocade embroidery chart

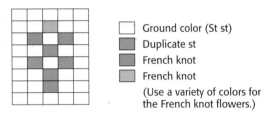

☐ Ground color (St st)
◼ Duplicate st
◼ French knot
◼ French knot
(Use a variety of colors for the French knot flowers.)

Hat Instructions

The hat has 2 options for finishing the lower edge. The first is a simple seed st edge. The second features the beaded BO used on the blanket.

Option 1: Seed Stitch Edge

With Chocolate and 16" circular needle in size 4, CO 90 sts. Join into rnd, being careful not to twist sts, and PM. Work in seed st for 5 rnds as follows:

Rnd 1: *K1, P1, rep from * around.

Rnd 2: *P1, K1, rep from * around.

End with rnd 1.

Change to 16" circular needle in size 6 and work rnds 1–18 of diamond brocade below.

Diamond Brocade

Rnd 1: *K9, P1, K8, rep from * around.

Rnds 2 and 18: *K8, P1, K1, P1, K7, rep from * around.

Rnds 3 and 17: *K7, P1, K3, P1, K6, rep from * around.

Rnds 4 and 16: *K6, P1, K5, P1, K5, rep from * around.

Rnds 5 and 15: *K5, P1, K7, P1, K4, rep from * around.

Rnds 6 and 14: *K4, P1, K9, P1, K3, rep from * around.

Rnds 7 and 13: *K3, P1, K11, P1, K2, rep from * around.

Rnds 8 and 12: *K2, P1, K13, P1, K1, rep from * around.

Rnds 9 and 11: *K1, P1, K15, P1, rep from * around.

Rnd 10: *P1, K17, rep from * around.

Purl 1 rnd.

Knit 1 rnd.

SHAPE CROWN

Next rnd: *K8, K2tog, rep from * around—81 sts.

Next rnd: Knit.

Next rnd: *K7, K2tog, rep from * around—72 sts.

Next rnd: Knit.

Cont in this manner, alternating a dec rnd with a plain rnd, and working 1 less st before dec on each subsequent dec rnd, until you've completed the *K2, K2tog rnd. From this point forward, omit the plain rnds between dec rnds. Cont as established, dec every rnd, until you've completed the *K2tog rnd. (Change to size 6 dpn when necessary).

Break yarn, thread through tapestry needle, and draw through rem sts. Weave in ends.

With yarns in contrasting colors, work embroidery in center of diamonds as shown in embroidery chart on page 32.

Option 2: Beaded Bind Off

Work as for option 1, but CO with 16" circular needle in size 6 and proceed immediately to working diamond brocade, omitting the 5 rnds seed st at the lower edge.

After completing crown of hat, work beaded BO along lower CO edge as follows:

With RS facing and with 16" circular needle in size 4, PU 89 sts along CO edge.

Purl 1 rnd.

Knit 1 rnd.

Turn work (you should be looking at the inside of the hat, with the yarn coming off the first st on the left-hand needle). Sl first st on the left-hand needle onto the right-hand needle. Work beaded BO (see page 8).

Booties Instructions

Again, you have 2 options: a simple rolled cuff or a beaded BO cuff.

Option 1: Rolled Cuff

With Chocolate and size 4 dpns, CO 22 sts. Do not join. Starting with a purl row, work 4 rows St st. Divide sts over 4 dpns, join into rnd, PM, and knit 2 rnds.

HEEL

K16, turn and purl across same 10 sts—these are heel sts. Place rem 12 sts on holder.

Knit 10 rows, ending with a WS row.

TURN HEEL

Row 1: K5, K2tog, K1.

Row 2: K2, K2tog, K1.

Row 3: K3, K2tog, K1.

Row 4: K4, K2tog, K1—6 sts. Break yarn.

GUSSET

Sl first 3 heel sts onto dpn. PM to mark beg of rnd and rejoin B. K3, PU 5 sts along selvage of heel flap, PM (this will be a "gusset marker"), K2, SSK, K4, K2tog, K2 from holder, PM (another "gusset marker"), PU 5 sts along other heel flap selvage, knit last 3 heel sts—26 sts.

SHAPE GUSSET

Next rnd: Purl to 2 sts before first gusset marker, P2tog. Knit to next gusset marker, P2tog, purl to end of rnd—24 sts.

Next rnd: Knit.

Rep these 2 rnds until there are 20 sts rem.

FOOT

Rnd 1: P5, K10, P5.

Rnd 2: Knit.

Rep these 2 rnds 5 times total—10 rnds.

SHAPE TOE

Next rnd: P3, P2tog, SSK, K6, K2tog, P2tog, P3—16 sts.

Next rnd: Knit.

Next rnd: P2, P2tog, SSK, K4, K2tog, P2tog, P2— 12 sts.

Break yarn, thread through tapestry needle, and draw through rem sts. Weave in ends.

With yarn in contrasting colors, work bootie embroidery, centered on top of foot. Refer to embroidery chart on page 32.

Option 2: Beaded Bind Off

Work as for option 1, replacing the 4 St st rows immediately after CO with 2 knit rows. Proceed with the patt as written.

After completing the bootie, work beaded BO along CO edge as follows:

With RS facing, PU 21 sts along CO edge.

Work beaded BO (page 8). There is no need to use smaller needles for this edge because the small number of stitches will keep the edge from flaring.

Using Leftover Yarn

If you buy full skeins of all the embroidery colors, you can use your leftovers for an additional hat and booties set.

Flowers

Here's a set of lovely projects for a baby born in the springtime.
Appliquéd flowers, leaves, and French knots add color and whimsy to
the simple stockinette stitch blanket. The Irish moss stitch borders are
worked as you go, simplifying finishing. The matching hat and
booties work up quickly and also incorporate floral appliqué.

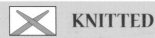 **KNITTED**

Finished Sizes

Blanket: 28" x 34"

Hat: Newborn (6 Months, 1 Year, 2 Years)
14¾ (16, 17½, 18¾)" circumference

Booties: 0–6 Months

Blanket Materials

- All Seasons Cotton from Rowan (60% cotton, 40% acrylic microfiber; 50 g; 90 m) in the following colors (**4**):

A	7 skeins	203 Giddy
B	1 skein	218 Pansy
C	1 skein	216 Citron
D	1 skein	205 Cheery
E	1 skein	217 Lime Leaf

- 24" circular needle in size 7 (4.5 mm), or size required to obtain gauge
- Tapestry needle
- 1¼ yards of preshrunk cotton fabric, at least 36" wide
- Sewing needle
- Sewing thread

Hat and Booties Materials

- 1 skein of All Seasons Cotton from Rowan (60% cotton, 40% acrylic microfiber; 50 g; 90 m), color 203 Giddy (**4**)
- Small amount of contrast yarn for embellishments
- Size 7 (4.5 mm) double-pointed needles
- Tapestry needle
- **For hat:** 16" circular needle in size 7 (4.5 mm), stitch marker
- **For booties:** Stitch holder or waste yarn, stitch markers

Gauge

18 sts and 28 rows = 4" in St st

Irish Moss Stitch

(Even-numbered rows are RS rows.)

Rows 1 and 2: K1, *P1, K1, rep from * across.

Rows 3 and 4: P1, *K1, P1, rep from * across.

Blanket Instructions

Lower Border

With A and 24" circular needle in size 7, CO 127 sts. Work 4 rows of Irish moss st.

Blanket

Row 1 (WS): (K1, P1) 2 times, purl to last 4 sts, (P1, K1) 2 times.

Row 2: (K1, P1) 2 times, knit to last 4 sts, (P1, K1) 2 times.

Row 3: (P1, K1) 2 times, purl to last 4 sts, (K1, P1) 2 times.

Row 4: (P1, K1) 2 times, knit to last 4 sts, (K1, P1) 2 times.

Rep these 4 rows until blanket measures 33" from CO, ending with row 4.

Upper Border

Work rows 1–4 of Irish moss st.

Next row: Work row 1 of patt one more time, binding off as you go.

Keeping Your Place in the Border

To keep your place when working the Irish moss stitch border, remember that on right-side rows you knit the purls and purl the knits, while on wrong-side rows you knit the knits and purl the purls.

Finishing

Make 1 big flower and 1 small flower with each of B, C, and D (or make as many flowers as you like).

With E, make several pairs of big and small leaves.

Appliqué flowers to blanket, filling in as needed with big and small leaves as shown. Add a French knot to the center of the flowers, and clusters of French knots to the base of the leaves (see page 12 for making French knots).

Line blanket (see page 12).

Big Flower

CO 3 sts.

Row 1 and all WS rows: Purl.

Row 2: (K1f&b) 2 times, K1—5 sts.

Rows 4 and 6: K1f&b, knit to last 2 sts, K1f&b, K1—9 sts.

Row 8: Knit.

Row 10: K3, sl2tog kw, K1, p2sso, K3—7 sts.

Row 12: K2, sl2tog kw, K1, p2sso, K2—5 sts.

Row 14: K1, sl2tog kw, K1, p2sso, K1—3 sts.

Break yarn, leaving a 6" tail. Place petal on holder.

Make 4 more petals. Leave yarn attached to the last petal. Transfer all petals onto one needle with RS facing you, and with the petal with the yarn still attached on the far left. Turn and work as follows:

P2, *P2tog, P1, rep from * across to last 4 sts, P2tog, P2—11 sts.

Break yarn, leaving a 10" tail. Thread through tapestry needle and draw through rem sts.

Block flower flat. Use tails in center to sew the inner sides of the petals together. Weave in these ends.

Securing the Flowers

When sewing down flowers and making French knots, use knots on the wrong side of the blanket to secure yarn rather than weaving in ends. Weaving alone may not be enough to keep the flowers in place.

Small Flower

CO 3 sts.

Row 1 and all WS rows: Purl.

Row 2: (K1f&b) 2 times, K1—5 sts.

Row 4: K1f&b, knit to last 2 sts, K1f&b, K1—7 sts.

Row 6: Knit.

Row 8: K2, sl2tog kw, K1, p2sso, K2—5 sts.

Row 10: K1, sl2tog kw, K1, p2sso, K1—3 sts.

Finish as for big flower.

Big (Small) Leaf

Make a petal as for big (small) flower through row 14 (10). At the end of row 14 (10), turn work, P3tog, break yarn, and fasten off.

Embellishment Options

You could omit the leaves and instead add a purl stitch or embroidered monogram to this blanket, or keep the flowers and add the monogram to just one corner.

Hat Instructions

With Giddy (referred to as yarn A for blanket) and 16" circular needle in size 7, CO 66 (72, 78, 84) sts. Join into rnd, being careful not to twist sts, and PM.

Knit 4 rnds for rolled edge.

Next rnd: *K1, P1, rep from * around.

Next 2 rnds: *P1, K1, rep from * around.

Next rnd: *K1, P1, rep from * around.

Work in St st until hat measures 3¼ (3½, 3¾, 4)" from beg of rolled edge.

Shape Crown

Next rnd: *K9 (10, 11, 12), K2tog, rep from * around—60 (66, 72, 78) sts.

Next rnd: Knit.

Next rnd: *K8 (9, 10, 11), K2tog, rep from * around—54 (60, 66, 72) sts.

Next rnd: Knit.

Next rnd: *K7 (8, 9, 10), K2tog, rep from * around—48 (54, 60, 66) sts.

Next rnd: Knit.

Cont as established, working 1 less st before the dec with each dec rnd and changing to size 7 dpn when necessary, until you've completed the *K6 (7, 8, 9), K2tog* rnd. From this point forward, omit plain rnd between dec rnds. Cont to dec every rnd until you've completed the *K2tog* rnd—6 sts. Break yarn, thread through tapestry needle, and draw through rem sts. Weave in ends.

Make a big and small leaf as for blanket and sew to side of hat. Add French knots.

Booties Instructions

With color of your choice and size 7 dpn, CO 19 sts.

Work K1, *P1, K1, rep from * for 4 rows.

Divide sts over 4 dpns, join into a circle, PM, and knit 1 rnd. At the same time, at the end of this rnd,

knit the last st of the rnd tog with the first st of second rnd—18 sts rem. Reposition marker so that the K2tog is the first st of the rnd.

Heel

K8, turn and purl across same 8 sts—these 8 are heel sts. Place rem 10 sts on holder or waste yarn.

Work in St st for 4 rows, ending with a WS row.

Turn Heel

Row 1: K5, K2tog, K1.

Row 2: P4, P2tog tbl, P1—6 sts.

Gusset

K3, PM to mark beg of rnd, K3 sts, PU 3 sts along selvage of heel flap, PM (this will be a "gusset marker"), K1, SSK, K4, K2tog, K1 from holder, PM (another "gusset marker"), PU 3 sts along other heel flap selvage, knit last 3 heel sts—20 sts.

Shape Gusset

Next rnd: Knit to 2 sts before first gusset marker, K2tog, knit to next gusset marker, SSK, knit to end of rnd—18 sts.

Next rnd: Knit.

Rep these 2 rnds 1 more time—16 sts.

Knit 7 rnds.

Shape Toe

Next rnd: K2, K2tog, SSK, K4, K2tog, SSK, K2—12 sts.

Next rnd: Knit.

Next rnd: K1, K2tog, SSK, K2, K2tog, SSK, K1—8 sts.

Break yarn, thread through tapestry needle, and draw through rem sts. Weave in ends.

Make a small leaf. Sew to top of bootie. With 2 other contrast colors, make 3 French knots at top of leaf.

Quack!

Colorful ducks and pretty stitch details combine to create a
lively design that's fun to knit and a pleasure to give.

 KNITTED

Finished Sizes

Blanket: 30" x 31½"

Hat: Newborn (6–12 Months, 1–2 Years)
15 (16½, 18)" circumference

Booties: 0–6 Months

Blanket Materials

- Wool Cotton from Rowan (50% merino wool, 50% cotton; 50 g; 123 yds) in the following colors **3**:

A	7 skeins	955 Ship Shape
B	3 skeins	901 Citron
C	1 skein	911 Rich

- 24" circular needle in size 3 (3.25 mm)
- 24" circular needle in size 5 (3.75 mm)
- Tapestry needle
- 1 yard of preshrunk cotton fabric, at least 36" wide
- Sewing needle
- Sewing thread

Hat and Booties Materials

- Wool Cotton from Rowan (50% merino wool, 50% cotton; 50 g; 123 yds) in the following colors **3**:

  Leftover yarn from blanket or 1 skein each of blanket yarns A, B, and C

- Size 5 (3.75 mm) double-pointed needles
- Stitch markers
- Tapestry needle
- **For hat:** 16" circular needle in size 3 (3.25 mm), 16" circular needle in size 5 (3.75 mm)
- **For booties:** Stitch holder or waste yarn

Gauge

24 sts and 28 rows = 4" over duck chart on size 5 needle

Seed Stitch Worked Flat (for Blanket)

All rows: K1, *P1, K1, rep from * across row.

Seed Stitch in the Round (for Hat)

Rnd 1: K1, *P1, K1, rep from * around.
Rnd 2: P1, *K1, P1, rep from * around.

Blanket Instructions

Lower Border

With 24" circular needle in size 3 and A, CO 185 sts. Work in seed st for 5 rows.

Change to size 5 circular needle and work 4 rows in St st, starting with a knit row.

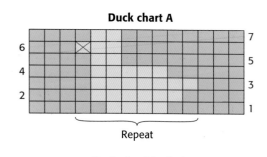

Duck chart A

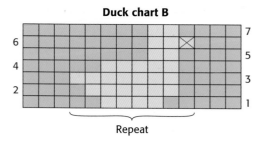

Duck chart B

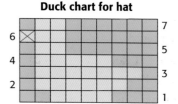

Duck chart for hat

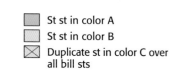

St st in color A
St st in color B
Duplicate st in color C over all bill sts

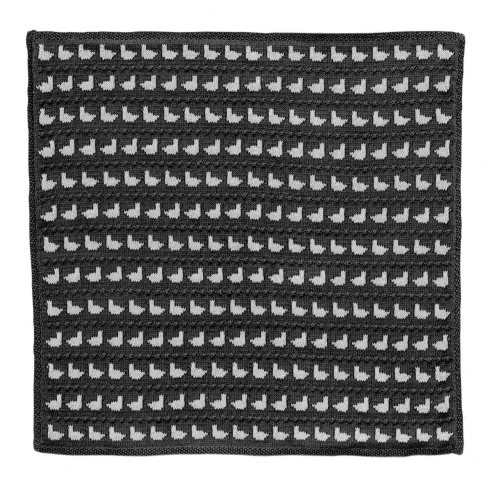

Pattern Sequence

Work rows 1–7 of duck chart A, 20 times across row.

Work 4 rows in St st, starting with a purl row.

Next row (WS): P2, K1, *P3tog, leaving sts on left needle, YO (wrapping yarn completely around needle), purl same 3 sts tog again, letting sts drop from left needle this time, K1, rep from *, end P2.

Work 4 rows in St st, starting with a knit row.

Work rows 1–7 of duck chart B across row.

Work 4 rows in St st, starting with a purl row.

Next row (WS): P2, K1, *P3tog, leaving sts on left needle, YO (wrapping yarn completely around needle), purl same 3 sts tog again, letting sts drop from left needle this time, K1, rep from *, end P2.

Work 4 rows in St st, starting with a knit row.

(End of pattern sequence)

Rep entire pattern sequence 5 more times.

Work rows 1–7 of duck chart A 1 more time. You should now have 13 rows of ducks total.

Work 4 rows in St st, starting with a purl row.

Change to size 3 needle and work 5 rows in seed st, BO on 5th row.

Side Borders

With the RS facing, size 3 needle, and A, PU 3 sts for every 4 rows along side of blanket, making sure you have an odd number of sts picked up. Work 5 rows in seed st, BO on 5th row.

Rep on 2nd side.

Block blanket.

Weave in ends.

Duplicate st duck bills in C as shown on chart (see page 40).

Line blanket (see page 12).

Hat Instructions

With 16" circular needle in size 3 and A, CO 89 (99, 107) sts. Join into rnd, being careful not to twist work, and PM.

Work 5 rnds in seed st.

Change to size 16" circular needle in size 5 and knit 2 rnds. AT THE SAME TIME, inc 1 (0, 1) st at end of first knit rnd—90 (99, 108) sts.

Make Ducks

Rep duck chart for hat around—you should have 10 (11, 12) ducks going around the hat.

After completing duck chart, knit 5 rnds.

Purl 1 rnd.

Change to C and knit 1 rnd.

Shape Crown

Next rnd: *K8 (9, 10), K2tog, rep from * around—81 (90, 99) sts.

Next rnd: Knit.

Next rnd: *K7 (8, 9), K2tog, rep from * around—72 (81, 90) sts.

Next rnd: Knit.

Cont in this manner, alternating a dec rnd with a plain rnd, and working 1 less st before dec on each subsequent dec rnd, until you've completed the *K2tog* rnd—9 sts. (Change to size 5 dpn when necessary.)

Knit 1 rnd.

Next rnd: *Sl2tog kw, K1, p2sso, rep from * around—3 sts.

Sl these 3 sts onto first dpn so that your yarn is coming off the far left st. Work I-cord for 1" (see page 9).

Next rnd: Sl2tog kw, K1, p2sso—1 st. Break yarn, and pull tail through st to fasten off. Weave in ends.

Duplicate st duck bills with C.

Booties Instructions

With A and size 5 dpns, CO 23 sts. Work 4 rows seed st.

Divide sts over 4 dpns, join into rnd, PM, and knit 2 rnds. AT THE SAME TIME, at the end of first rnd, knit last st of rnd tog with first st of second

rnd—22 sts. Reposition marker so that K2tog is first st of rnd.

At end of second rnd, break A.

Heel

Sl first 6 sts onto a st holder or waste yarn. Join C, K10, turn and purl across same 10 sts—these are heel sts. Place rem 6 sts on same holder or waste yarn as first 6 sts.

Work in St st for 8 rows, ending with a WS row.

Turn Heel

Row 1: K5, K2tog, K1.

Row 2: P2, P2tog tbl, P1.

Row 3: K3, K2tog, K1.

Row 4: P4, P2tog tbl, P1—6 sts. Break C.

Gusset

Sl first 3 heel sts onto dpn. PM to mark beg of rnd and rejoin A. K3, PU 5 sts along selvage of heel flap, PM (this will be a "gusset marker"), K2, SSK, K4, K2tog, K2 from holder, PM (another "gusset marker"), PU 5 sts along other heel flap selvage, knit last 3 heel sts—26 sts.

Shape Gusset

Next rnd: Knit to 2 sts before first gusset marker, K2tog, knit to next gusset marker, SSK, knit to end of rnd—24 sts.

Next rnd: Knit.

Rep these 2 rnds until 20 sts rem.

Knit 10 rnds. Break A at end of 10th rnd.

Shape Toe

Join C.

Next rnd: Knit.

Next rnd: K3, K2tog, SSK, K6, K2tog, SSK, K3—16 sts.

Next rnd: Knit.

Next rnd: K2, K2tog, SSK, K4, K2tog, SSK, K2—12 sts.

Break yarn, thread through tapestry needle, and draw through rem sts.

Duplicate st duck on front of foot.

Woven Stripes

Here's a simple design for a warm and cozy blanket. Although the pattern is somewhat dense, the blanket has a soft hand and pleasing drape. The matching hat and booties complete the set.

 CROCHETED

Finished Sizes

Blanket: 33" x 31¼"

Hat: Newborn (0–6 Months, 1 Year, 2 Years)
14 (15¼, 17½, 18½)" circumference

Booties: 0–6 Months

Blanket Materials

- Cotton Cashmere from Debbie Bliss (85% cotton, 15% cashmere; 50 g; 95 m) in the following colors **❸** :

A	4 skeins	19 Fuchsia
B	4 skeins	03 Cream
C	4 skeins	18 Magenta

- Size H-8 (5 mm) crochet hook
- Tapestry needle

Hat and Booties Materials

- Cotton Cashmere from Debbie Bliss (85% cotton, 15% cashmere; 50 g; 95 m) in the following colors **❸** :

  1 additional skein of each color used for blanket will make both the hat and booties.
- Size H-8 (5 mm) crochet hook
- Tapestry needle

Gauge

22 sts and 21 rows = 4" in woven st

Woven Stitch for Blanket

Ch-1 sps count as a st when working woven st.

Rows 1 and 2: With A, ch 2, sk first sc, *1 sc in ch-1 sp, ch 1, rep from * across, ending with 1 sc in tch sp.

Rows 3 and 4: With B, ch 2, sk first sc, *1 sc in ch-1 sp, ch 1, rep from * across, ending with 1 sc in tch sp.

Rows 5 and 6: With C, ch 2, sk first sc, *1 sc in ch-1 sp, ch 1, rep from * across, ending with 1 sc in tch sp.

Rep these 6 rows for patt.

(See page 10 for how to change colors when crocheting.)

Handling Colors

Colors may be carried up the side of the work rather than broken at each color change. Just be sure to leave a long enough "float" from the carried color to avoid any puckering along the side selvage.

Blanket Instructions

With A, ch 183.

Set-up row (counts as row 1 of patt the first time through only): Sk first 2 chs, sc in next ch, *ch 1, sk 1 ch, sc in next ch, rep from * across—182 sts.

Beg woven st for blanket, starting with row 2 (set-up row counted as row 1). Work rows 1–6 of patt 27 times.

Work rows 1 and 2 one more time. Break yarn and fasten off. Weave in ends.

Hat Instructions

Shape Crown

With C, ch 2. Work 6 sc in second ch from hook, PM in first sc worked. Do not turn.

Rnd 1: 2 sc in marked st. This will join work into a circle. 2 sc in next 5 sts—12 sts.

PM in last st of rnd. Move marker to last st of each subsequent rnd.

Rnd 2: *Sc in next st, 2 sc in next st; rep from * around—18 sts.

Rnd 3: *Sc in next 2 sts, 2 sc in next st; rep from * around—24 sts.

Rnd 4: *Sc in next 3 sts, 2 sc in next st; rep from * around—30 sts.

Rnd 5: *Sc in next 4 sts, 2 sc in next st; rep from * around—36 sts.

Rnd 6: *Sc in next 5 sts, 2 sc in next st; rep from * around—42 sts.

Rnd 7: *Sc in next 6 sts, 2 sc in next st; rep from * around—48 sts.

Rnd 8: *Sc in next 7 sts, 2 sc in next st; rep from * around—54 sts.

Rnd 9: *Sc in next 8 sts, 2 sc in next st; rep from * around—60 sts.

Cont in this manner, inc 6 sts per rnd, until you complete rnd 11 (12, 14, 15) as follows: *Sc in next 11 (12, 14, 15) sts, 2 sc in next st; rep from * around—78 (84, 96, 102) sts.

Sides

With A, work set-up rnd (counts as rnd 1): Ch 2, *sk next sc, 1 sc in next sc, ch 1, rep from * around, to last sc, sc in last sc.

Beg woven st, starting with rnd 2 first time through only.

Woven Stitch

Rnds 1 and 2: With A, ch 2, sc in ch sp from previous rnd, ch 1, *sk next sc, 1 sc in ch-1 sp, ch 1, rep from * around, ending with 1 sc last ch sp.

Rnds 3 and 4: With B, ch 2, sc in ch sp from previous rnd, ch 1, *sk next sc, 1 sc in ch-1 sp, ch 1, rep from * around, ending with 1 sc last ch sp.

Rnds 5 and 6: With C, ch 2, sc in ch sp from previous rnd, ch 1, *sk next sc, 1 sc in ch-1 sp, ch 1, rep from * around, ending with 1 sc last ch sp.

Work rnds 1–6 two times. Break yarns and fasten off. Weave in ends.

Booties Instructions

Toe

When making booties, change colors every 2 rnds, following stripe sequence until you reach the heel. Heel is then worked solid in the next color of the stripe sequence.

With A, ch 2. Work 6 sc in second ch from hook, PM in first sc worked. Do not turn.

Rnd 1: With A, 2 sc in marked st. This will join work into a rnd. 2 sc in next 5 sts—12 sts.

PM in last st of rnd. Move marker to last st of each subsequent rnd.

Rnd 2: *With B, sc in next 5 sts, 2 sc in next st, rep from * around—14 sts.

Rnd 3: *With B, sc in next 6 sts, 2 sc in next st, rep from * around—16 sts.

Rnd 4: *With C, sc in next 7 sts, 2 sc in next st, rep from * around—18 sts.

Rnd 5: With C, sc around.

Rnds 6 and 7: With A, sc around.

Rnds 8 and 9: With B, sc around.

At the end of rnd 9, break all yarns and fasten off. You may want to weave in your ends at this point, because it will be easier to do now than when the bootie is finished.

Heel

Use color C for remainder of bootie.

PM where you want top center of foot to be (position marker so that original start of rnd is on bottom of foot). Join next color in sequence 2 sts to left of marker.

Sc in next 14 sts, turn.

(Ch 1, sc in next 14 sts, turn) for 2 rows.

Ch 1, sc in next 4 sts, (sc2tog) 3 times, sc in last 4 sts, turn—11 sts.

Ch 1, sc 11, turn.

Ch 1, sc in next 4 sts, sc3tog, sc in last 4 sts, turn—9 sts.

Ch 1, sc 9. Break yarn and fasten off.

Sew center back heel seam.

With RS facing, rejoin heel color yarn at center back heel, and sc 2 rows around foot opening. Finish the last rnd by joining the last st of rnd to the first st of rnd with a sl st or with duplicate st join (see page 11). Break yarn and fasten off.

Granny Squares

Made with a variant of the traditional crocheted granny square, this colorful blanket makes a wonderful group project. Friends and family members can each crochet a few squares, and even non-crocheters can help sew the squares together. The matching hat and booties are adorable additions.

CROCHETED

Finished Sizes

Blanket: 29½" x 29½"

Hat: Newborn (0–6 Months, 1–2 Years)
14¾ (16½, 18½)" circumference

Booties: 0–6 Months

Blanket Materials

♦ Handknit Cotton from Rowan (100% cotton; 50 g; 93 yds) in the following colors (4):

A	2 skeins	263 Bleached
B	2 skeins	310 Shell
C	2 skeins	203 Fruit Salad
D	2 skeins	303 Sugar
E	2 skeins	219 Gooseberry
F	2 skeins	315 Double Chocolate
G	2 skeins	307 Spanish Red

♦ Size H-8 (5 mm) crochet hook
♦ Tapestry needle
♦ **Optional:** 1 yard of preshrunk cotton fabric, at least 36" wide; sewing needle; sewing thread

Hat and Booties Materials

♦ Handknit Cotton from Rowan (100% cotton; 50 g; 93 yds) in the following colors (4):

Leftover yarn from blanket or small amounts of yarn in a variety of colors
♦ Size H-8 (5 mm) crochet hook
♦ Tapestry needle

Gauge

13 sts and 8 rnds = 4" in dc with size H-8 crochet hook

Each square measures approximately 4" x 4".

Basic Square

Ch 4, join last ch to first ch with sl st to form a ring.

Rnd 1: Ch 3 (counts as 1 dc), 2 dc in ring, (ch 1, 3 dc in ring) 3 times, ch 1, join with sl st in top of starting ch 3. Break yarn.

Rnd 2: With RS facing, join next color in any ch-1 sp. Ch 3 (counts as 1 dc), 4 dc in same sp for corner, 1 dc between 2nd and 3rd st of next 3 dc group, (5 dc in next ch-1 sp, 1 dc between 2nd and 3rd st of next 3 dc group) 3 times, join last st of rnd to top of starting ch 3 with sl st. Break yarn.

Rnd 3: With RS facing, join next color between 3rd and 4th sts of any corner group. Ch 3 (counts as 1 dc), 5 dc in same sp for corner, (3 dc in next single dc, 6 dc between 3rd and 4th sts of next corner group) 3 times, 3 dc in next single dc, join last st of rnd to top of starting ch 3 with sl st. Break yarn.

Rnd 4: With RS facing, join next color between third and fourth sts of any corner group. Ch 3 (counts as 1 dc), 5 dc in same sp, 3 dc between fifth and sixth sts of same corner group, (3 dc between second and third sts of next 3 dc group, 3 dc between first and second sts of next corner group, 6 dc between third and fourth sts of same corner group, 3 dc between fifth and sixth sts of same corner group) 3 times, 3 dc between second and third sts of next 3 dc group, 3 dc between first and second sts of next corner group, join last st of rnd to starting ch 3 with sl st. Break yarn. Weave in ends.

Blanket Instructions

Make 49 blocks in color sequences indicated on chart.

Finishing

Sew blocks tog in sequence shown on chart or as desired.

To sew, use yarn in either color of the outer edges of the 2 blocks being sewn tog. Sew 9 to 10 sts from each block, joining along the center 3 dc clusters. (See page 11 for sewing how-tos.)

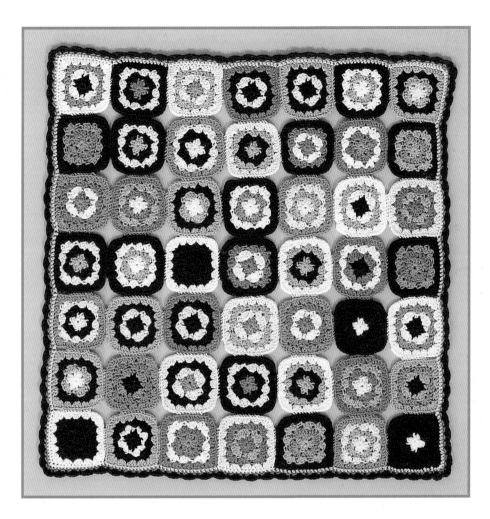

Granny square blanket chart

F A E A	D F B F	E B C B	F B F D	G B G C	A C A F	B C F C
E D E F	C G B G	B F B E	C F C B	D A D G	E D A D	C E C G
D A D E	B D C D	A C G C	A E A F	B C B E	F A C A	D C D B
C G B G	A C A F	G F G A	D A D G	C G C A	G D A D	E D E F
B F B E	G B G C	F B F D	E B C B	D A D E	A G F G	F A E A
A C G C	F E D E	E B F B	D F B F	C G C A	B D C D	G C E C
G F G A	F A F C	E D A D	D C D B	C E C G	B C B E	A G F G

Colors are listed from left to right in the order they are used in each square. For example, the starting color for the square in the upper left corner of the chart is F, the next color is A, then E, and then A.

Work edging as follows:

Rnd 1: With RS facing, join B at any corner between third and fourth sts. *Sc 3 in corner sp, sc 15 sts along sides of next 7 squares, rep from * around, end by joining last sc to first sc with a sl st. Break B and fasten off.

Rnd 2: With RS facing, join D between the second and third sc of any corner group. *Sc 3 in corner st, sc 16 sts along sides of same square, 15 sts along the sides of the next 5 squares, 16 sts along side of next square, rep from * around, end by joining last sc to first sc with a sl st. Break D and fasten off.

Rnd 3: With RS facing, join G between the 2nd and 3rd sc of any corner group. Ch 3, 2 dc in corner st, (sc in next sc, *sk 1 sc, 3 dc in next sc, sk 1 sc, sc in next sc, rep from * to corner, 3 dc in corner) 3 times, sc in next sc, **sk 1 sc, 3 dc in next sc, sk 1 sc, sc in next sc, rep from ** to start of rnd. End by joining last sc to top of starting ch with a sl st. Break G and fasten off. Weave in rem ends.

Design Options

♦ The Granny Squares blanket can easily be sized up or down simply by making more or fewer squares.

♦ Using variegated yarn will create multicolored effects without requiring you to change colors with each row.

♦ Repeat the same square 49 times for the entire blanket. Done in a subdued palette, this will create a subtle counterpoint to the bold version shown here.

♦ If you are concerned about little fingers and toes poking through the spaces between the squares, adding a colorful lining solves the problem and adds pizzazz to the blanket. You can also sew the squares together a bit more tightly to minimize the spaces between them.

Hat Instructions

Each rnd of the hat is worked in a different color (see page 10 for more information on changing colors). I like to randomly sequence the yarns as I go, rather than planning the color placement ahead of time. That way, each hat is unique.

Using rem yarn from blanket, follow instructions for basic square through rnd 3—36 sts at end of rnd 3.

Rnd 4: With RS facing, join next color between the 3rd and 4th sts of any corner group, ch 3 (counts as 1 dc), dc in next 4 sts, 2 dc in next dc, *dc in next 5 sts, 2 dc in next st, rep from * around. Join last st of rnd to top of tch with sl st—42 sts.

Rnd 5: Ch 3 (counts as 1 dc), dc in next 5 sts, 2 dc in next st, *dc in next 6 sts, 2 dc in next st, rep from * around. Join last st of rnd to top of tch with sl st—48 sts. Size Newborn, go to **.

Rnd 6: Ch 3 (counts as 1 dc), dc in next 6 sts, 2 dc in next st, *dc in next 7 sts, 2 dc in next st, rep from * around. Join last st of rnd to top of tch with sl st—54 sts. Size 0–6 Months, go to **.

Rnd 7: Ch 3 (counts as 1 dc), dc in next 7 sts, 2 dc in next st, *dc in next 8 sts, 2 dc in next st, rep from * around. Join last st of rnd to top of tch with sl st 60 sts. Size 1–2 Years, go to **.

**Cont to work in dc rnds without inc, cont to change colors with every rnd until hat measures approximately 5 (5½, 6)" from the top.

Finishing

Sc 2 rnds, changing color with each rnd. Break yarn and fasten off.

Weave in all ends.

Booties Instructions

Toe

With first color, ch 2. Work 6 sc in second ch from hook, PM in first sc worked. Do not turn.

Rnd 1: 2 sc in marked st. This will join work into a circle. 2 sc in next 5 sts—12 sts.

PM in last st of rnd. Move marker to last st of each subsequent rnd.

Rnd 2: *Sc in next 5 sts, 2 sc in next st, rep from * around—14 sts.

Rnd 3: *Sc in next 6 sts, 2 sc in next st, rep from * around, joining second color in last st of rnd—16 sts. Break first color.

Rnd 4: *Sc in next 7 sts, 2 sc in next st, rep from * around—18 sts.

Sc 5 rnds even.

Heel

Sc in first 7 sts, turn. Remove marker at this point.

(Ch 1, sc in next 14 sts, turn) 2 times.

Ch 1, sc in next 4 sts, (sc2tog) 3 times, sc in last 4 sts, turn—11 sts.

Ch 1, sc 11, turn.

Ch 1, sc in next 4 sts, sc3tog, sc in last 4 sts, turn—9 sts.

Ch 1, sc 9. Break yarn and fasten off.

Sew center back heel seam.

With RS facing, rejoin 2nd color at center back heel and sc around foot opening. Join 3rd color and sc 1 more rnd. Finish the last rnd by joining the last st of rnd to the first st of rnd with a sl st or with duplicate st join (see page 11). Break yarn and fasten off.

Weave in ends.

Bobble Edge Lace

This delicate and simple stitch pattern makes a lovely traditional baby set. The pattern, while easy, does take some time to knit, so this is a project you want to start well in advance of the baby shower.

KNITTED

Finished Sizes

Blanket: 27" x 27"*

Bonnet: 0–6 Months (6–18 Months)

Booties: 0–6 Months

This pattern looks good just as it comes off the needle or blocked to open up the lacework. Blocking the blanket will enlarge it to about 30" x 30".

Blanket Materials

♦ 5 skeins of Shepherd Sport from Lorna's Laces (100% superwash wool; 70 g; 200 yds), color Peach ❷

♦ 24" circular needle in size 4 (3.5 mm)

♦ Tapestry needle

Bonnet and Booties Materials

♦ 1 skein of Shepherd Sport from Lorna's Laces (100% superwash wool; 70 g; 200 yds), color Peach ❷

♦ **For bonnet:** 24" circular needle in size 4 (3.5 mm) or size 4 (3.5 mm) straight needles

♦ **For booties:** Size 4 (3.5 mm) double-pointed needles, stitch holder or waste yarn, stitch markers

♦ 50" length of ribbon, ½" wide

♦ Sewing needle

♦ Sewing thread

♦ Tapestry needle

Gauge

25 sts and 40 rows = 4" in open star st (unblocked)

Open Star Stitch

Row 1 (WS): K2, *YO, K3, insert left needle into first of K3 sts, and lift it over next 2 sts and off right needle, rep from * across to last st, K1.

Rows 2 and 4: Knit.

Row 3: K1, *K3, insert left needle into first of K3 sts, and lift it over next 2 sts and off right needle, YO, rep from * across to last 2 sts, K2.

Rep these 4 rows for patt.

Bobble Edge (Multiple of 3 + 2)

Row 1 (WS): K2, *knit into front, back, and front of same st (3 sts made out of 1), turn work, purl these 3 sts, turn work, K3tog, K2, rep from * across.

Row 2: BO in purl.

When worked along a cast on or bound off edge, the bobbles in the bobble edge should line up with yarn overs in the blanket. If you find you are off, you can fudge a bit by starting or ending the row with K1 or K3 (instead of the given K2) as the situation requires.

Blanket Instructions

With 24" circular needle in size 4, CO 168 sts.

Knit 1 row.

Work rows 1–4 of open star st until blanket measures 27". Work rows 1–2 one more time.

Upper Border

Work bobble edge, lining up bobbles with yarn overs of last row of blanket. There will be 1 blanket st left over at the end of row 1 of bobble edge—knit this st and proceed with row 2.

Lower Border

With RS facing, PU 167 sts. Work bobble edge, lining up bobbles with yarn overs in row 1 of blanket.

Side Borders

With RS facing, PU 167 sts along side. Work bobble edge.

Rep on 2nd side.

Weave in ends.

Block blanket as desired.

Bonnet Instructions

With 24" circular needle in size 4, CO 72 (84) sts.

Knit 1 row.

Work rows 1–4 of open star st 9 (11) times.

Size 0–6 Months

Next row: BO 24 sts, K1, (YO, K3, insert left needle into first of K3 sts, and lift it over next 2 sts and off right needle) 7 times, K1, BO rem 24 sts. Break yarn and rejoin with RS facing—24 sts.

Knit 1 row.

Next row: K1, *K3, insert left needle into first of K3 sts, and lift it over next 2 sts and off right needle, YO, rep from * to last 2 sts, K2.

Next row: Knit.

Next row: K2, *YO, K3, insert left needle into first of K3 sts, and lift it over next 2 sts and off right needle, rep from * to last st, K1.

Next row: Knit.

Rep the last 4 rows 7 more times, and then work the first 2 rows 1 more time, ending with a RS row completed. BO in knit on the next (WS) row. Go to "Finishing."

Size 6–18 Months

Next row: BO 28 sts, (K3, insert left needle into first of K3 sts, and lift it over next 2 sts and off right needle, YO) 8 times, K3, BO rem 28 sts. Break yarn and rejoin with RS facing—28 sts.

Knit 1 row.

Next row: K2, *YO, K3, insert left needle into first of K3 sts, and lift it over next 2 sts and off right needle, rep from * to last 2 sts, K2.

Next row: Knit.

Next row: K1, *K3, insert left needle into first of K3 sts, and lift it over next 2 sts and off right needle, YO, rep from * to last 3 sts, K3.

Next row: Knit.

Rep the last 4 rows 9 more times, and then work first 2 rows 1 more time, ending with a RS row completed. BO in knit on next (WS) row.

Finishing

Sew back seams.

Borders: With RS facing, PU 71 (83) sts along CO edge. Work bobble edge, lining up bobbles with yarn overs along CO edge. With RS facing, PU 65 (74) sts along lower edge. Work bobble edge.

Ties: Cut ribbon in half and attach to front corners.

Booties Instructions

With size 4 dpns, CO 24 sts. Knit 1 row.

Work rows 1–4 of open star st. Divide sts evenly over 3 dpns, join into rnd, and PM.

Knit 2 rnds.

Heel

K18, turn, and purl across same 12 sts—these are heel sts. Place rem 12 sts on holder.

Knit 10 rows, ending with a WS row.

Turn Heel

Row 1: K6, K2tog, K1.

Row 2: K2, K2tog, K1.

Row 3: K3, K2tog, K1.

Row 4: K4, K2tog, K1.

Row 5: K5, K2tog.

Row 6: K5, K2tog—6 sts.

Gusset

K3, PM to mark beg of rnd, K3, PU 5 sts along selvage of heel flap, PM (this will be a "gusset marker"), K2, SSK, K4, K2tog, K2 from holder, PM (another "gusset marker"), PU 5 sts along other heel flap selvage, knit last 3 heel sts—26 sts.

Shape Gusset

Next rnd: Knit to 2 sts before first gusset marker, K2tog. Knit to next gusset marker, SSK, knit to end of rnd—24 sts.

Next rnd: Knit.

Rep these 2 rnds until 20 sts rem. Knit 10 rnds.

Shape Toe

Next rnd: K3, K2tog, SSK, K6, K2tog, SSK, K3—16 sts.

Next rnd: Knit.

Next rnd: K2, K2tog, SSK, K4, K2tog, SSK, K2—12 sts.

Break yarn, thread through tapestry needle, and draw through rem sts.

Cuff

With RS facing, PU 23 sts along CO edge. Work bobble edge, lining up bobbles with yarn overs along CO. Weave in ends.

Rose Leaf

A project for the more experienced knitter, this blanket is worked from the center out in stockinette stitch; the lace border is then knit onto the live blanket stitches. The cap and booties use the same technique as the blanket. A charming ribbon accent completes the cap.

Finished Sizes

Blanket: 32" x 32" (blocked)

Cap: 0–6 Months (6–18 Months)

Booties: 0–6 Months

Blanket Materials

- 7 skeins of Cotton Patine from Elsebeth Lavold (100% cotton; 50 g; 110 m), color 12 Rosehip **3**
- Size 4 (3.5 mm) double-pointed needles
- 24" circular needle in size 4 (3.5 mm)
- Size 6 (4 mm) double-pointed needles
- 16" circular needle in size 6 (4 mm)
- 24" circular needle in size 6 (4 mm)
- Stitch marker

Cap Materials

- 1 skein of Cotton Patine from Elsebeth Lavold (100% cotton; 50 g; 110 m), color 12 Rosehip **3**
- Size 6 (4 mm) double-pointed needles
- 16" circular needle in size 6 (4 mm)
- Size 4 (3.5 mm) double-pointed needles
- 16" circular needle in size 4 (3.5 mm)

- 50" length of ribbon, ½" wide
- Stitch marker
- Tapestry needle

Booties Materials

- 1 skein of Cotton Patine from Elsebeth Lavold (100% cotton; 50 g; 110 m), color 12 Rosehip **3**
- Size 4 (3.5 mm) double-pointed needles
- Stitch markers
- Stitch holder or waste yarn
- Tapestry needle

Gauge

20 sts and 30 rows = 4" in St st on size 6 needle

Blanket Instructions

With size 6 dpn, CO 4 sts.

K1f&b into each st—8 sts.

Divide onto 4 dpns, placing 2 sts on each needle. Join into rnd, PM in first st of rnd.

Knit 1 rnd.

Next rnd: K1f&b in each st—16 sts.

Next rnd: Knit.

Next rnd: *K1f&b, K2, K1f&b, rep from * around—24 sts.

Next rnd: Knit.

Rose leaf edging chart

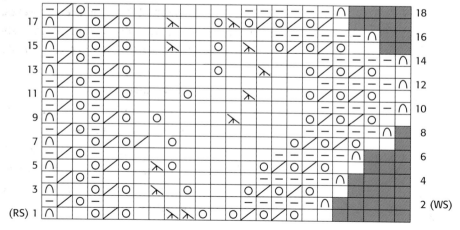

Knit on RS, purl on WS
Purl on RS, knit on WS
YO
K2tog
Sl1 kw, K2tog, psso
Sl1 pw wyif, and then move yarn between the needles to the back of the work for the next knit st
No st

Even-numbered rows are WS and worked from right to left.
RS rows are worked from left to right.

The last st of all WS (even-numbered) rows is worked as a K2tog with the next st of the blanket, unless otherwise indicated, such as when working corner edges (see text).

Next rnd: *K1f&b, K4, K1f&b, rep from * around—
32 sts.

Next rnd: Knit.

Next rnd: *K1f&b, K6, K1f&b, rep from * around—
40 sts.

Next rnd: Knit.

Next rnd: *K1f&b, K8, K1f&b, rep from * around—
48 sts.

Next rnd: Knit.

Next rnd: *K1f&b, K10, K1f&b, rep from * around—
56 sts.

Next rnd: Knit.

Cont in this manner, inc 8 sts every other rnd as
established, until you have 360 sts (90 sts per
side), and ending with a plain knit rnd. As blanket
gets bigger, you will be able to transfer sts to
16" circular in size 6, and then to 24" circular in
size 6.

Border

Transfer blanket sts to 24" circular needle in size 4 by
slipping them pw from size 6 needle.

Remove marker at start of rnd, and then knit first
st of rnd. This is a "corner st"—the st sitting
between the horizontal bars of the increases.
You need to be able to recognize the corner sts
when attaching the border, so take note of its
appearance.

Turn blanket so that WS is facing you.

Using a size 4 dpn and the left tip of the size 4 circular
needle, cable CO (see page 5) 19 sts.

Beg chart for rose leaf edging, starting with row 2
(first time through only), attaching border to
blanket as you go. Note that row 2 is a WS row
and is worked from right to left.

Attaching Lace Borders

The beauty of a knitted lace border is that it allows you to finish the edges of the blanket without having to bind off, while at the same time creating a dramatic finish for your project. The technique is simple—just follow the border chart, attaching the border to the blanket by knitting the last stitch of the wrong side border rows together with the next stitch of the blanket. The trick is rounding the blanket corners. On the straight sides of the blanket the border is attached to the blanket on each wrong side row (that is, every other row). But at the blanket corners, you need to attach the blanket on every fourth row to create the extra fabric that allows the border to gracefully curve around the corner. These extra rows are worked on each half of the corner. Without the extra border rows, the border pulls in, straining to make the curve. Below, I walk you through the first half corner row by row. You will repeat the process for each half corner.

First Half Corner Only

(This happens immediately after the initial cable CO.)

Work row 2 according to chart, knitting last chart st tog with corner st of blanket.

Rows 3, 4, and 5: Work according to chart, but do not attach row 4.

Row 6: Work according to chart, attaching row 6 to blanket.

Rows 7, 8, and 9: Work according to chart, but do not attach row 8.

Row 10: Work according to chart, attaching row 10 to blanket.

Rows 11, 12, and 13: Work according to chart, but do not attach row 12.

Row 14: Work according to chart, attaching row 13 to blanket.

Rows 15, 16, and 17: Work according to chart, but do not attach row 16.

Row 18: Work according to chart, attaching row 18 to blanket.

As you can see in the steps outlined below left, the border was attached on every fourth row, 4 times. You will need to work each of the rem 7 half corners in a similar manner to attach the border on every fourth row, 4 times.

After working the first half corner, cont with border chart along the straight sides, attaching every wrong side (even-numbered) row to the blanket, until you are 4 sts away from the next corner st. (As you approach a corner, you may want to PM in it to keep you on track.) When you are 4 sts from the corner st, cont the border patt as established, attaching the border on every fourth row, 4 times. Work the second half of the corner, also attaching the border on every fourth row, 4 times. Cont around, attaching every other border row on the straight sides and every fourth row on the corners, until you have worked all the way around the blanket. BO your last row, and sew the CO and bound-off edges of the border tog.

Tip

As you round the final half corner, you may want to do a bit of fudging to get the cast-on edge and the bound-off edge to match. The pattern doesn't have to line up perfectly; as long as the 2 edges are about the same length they should sew up neatly.

Block blanket into shape. Wet blocking will achieve the best results. Weave in ends.

Cap Instructions

With size 6 dpn, CO 4 sts.

K1f&b into each st—8 sts.

Divide onto 4 dpns, placing 2 sts on each needle. Join into rnd, PM in first st of rnd.

Knit 1 rnd.

Next rnd: K1f&b in each st—16 sts.

Next rnd: Knit.

Next rnd: *K1f&b, K1, rep from * around—24 sts.

Next rnd: Knit.

Next rnd: *K1f&b, K2, rep from * around—32 sts.

Next rnd: Knit.

Next rnd: *K1f&b, K3, rep from * around—40 sts.

Next rnd: Knit.

Next rnd: *K1f&b, K4, rep from * around—48 sts.

Next rnd: Knit.

Next rnd: *K1f&b, K5, rep from * around—56 sts.

Next rnd: Knit.

Cont in this manner, inc 8 sts every other rnd as established, until you have 64 (80) sts, ending with a plain knit rnd and changing to 16" circular needle in size 6 when possible.

Border

Transfer cap sts to 16" circular needle in size 4. Turn cap so that WS is facing you.

Using a size 4 dpn and left circular needle, cable CO (see page 5) 19 sts.

Beg chart for rose leaf edging (see page 56), starting with row 2 (first time through only), attaching border by knitting last st of every WS (even-numbered) row tog with next available cap st. Work rose leaf edging chart 5 (6) times. Work row 1 one more time.

Next row: BO first 18 border sts in knit, working last border st tog with next cap st—19 (26) sts rem after BO border [18 (25) cap sts on size 4 circular needle plus 1 st rem on dpn from BO].

BO rem sts with beaded BO (see page 8).

Thread ribbon through front edge of cap.

The rose leaf cap should be minimally blocked, if at all, because over blocking will make it too large.

Booties Instructions

CO 22 sts onto size 4 dpn. Divide sts over 4 dpns, join into rnd, PM, and knit 2 rnds.

Heel

K10, turn, and purl across same 10 sts—these are heel sts. Place rem 12 sts on holder.

Knit 10 rows, ending with a WS row.

Turn Heel

Row 1: K5, K2tog, K1.

Row 2: K2, K2tog, K1.

Row 3: K3, K2tog, K1.

Row 4: K4, K2tog, K1—6 sts.

Gusset

K3, PM to mark beg of rnd, K3, PU 5 sts along selvage of heel flap, PM (this will be a "gusset marker"), K2, SSK, K4, K2tog, K2 from holder, PM (another "gusset marker"), PU 5 sts along other heel flap selvage, knit last 3 heel sts—26 sts.

Shape Gusset

Next rnd: Knit to 2 sts before first gusset marker, K2tog. Knit to next gusset marker, SSK, knit to end of rnd—24 sts.

Next rnd: Knit.

Rep these 2 rnds until 20 sts rem.

Knit 10 rnds.

Shape Toe

Next rnd: K3, K2tog, SSK, K6, K2tog, SSK, K3—16 sts.

Next rnd: Knit.

Next rnd: K2, K2tog, SSK, K4, K2tog, SSK, K2—12 sts.

Break yarn, thread through tapestry needle, and draw through rem sts.

Turn bootie WS out. Starting at center front of foot, PU 20 sts around foot opening. Do not join. Cable CO 7 sts (see page 5 for cable CO).

Work following border and attach to bootie, starting with row 2 first time through only.

Bootie Edging

Row 1: Sl1 pw wyif, yarn to back between needles, K1, YO, K1, YO, K2.

Row 2: Sl1 pw wyif, yarn to back between needles, K5, knit last border st tog with next bootie st.

Row 3: Sl1 pw wyif, yarn to back between needles, K2, YO, K2tog, YO, K2.

Row 4: Sl1 pw wyif, yarn to back between needles, K6, knit last border st tog with next bootie st.

Row 5: Sl1 pw wyif, yarn to back between needles, K3, YO, K2tog, YO, K2.

Row 6: BO first 4 sts (still slipping first st pw wyif, yarn to back between needles), K3, knit last border st tog with first bootie st.

Rep these 6 rows until all the bootie sts have been worked—your last attaching row should be row 4. BO rem sts in knit on next row. Weave in ends.

Hat Instructions

With A and 16" circular needle in size 7, CO 136 (152) sts. Join into rnd, being careful not to twist sts, and PM.

Ruffle

Rnds 1–3: *P1, K3, rep from * around.

Rnd 4: *P1, sl2tog kw, K1, p2sso, rep from * around—68 (76) sts.

Change to B and knit 1 rnd.

Begin Pattern

Rnds 1 and 3: With B, *sl1 pw, K1, YO, pass slipped st over K1 and YO, rep from * around. Break B at end of rnd 3.

Rnd 2: With B, knit.

Rnd 4: With A, knit.

Rnd 5: With A, *K1f&b, K1, rep from * around—102 (114) sts.

Rnds 6–11: With A, knit.

Rnd 12: Rejoin B, *K1, K2tog, rep from * around—68 (76) sts.

Rep these 12 rnds for patt.

(Color A may be carried throughout rnds 1–12. Color B should be broken when not in use.)

Work rnds 1–12 two times, and then rnds 1–4 one more time.

Knit 3 (5) more rnds with A.

Change to size 7 dpn and beg crown shaping.

Next rnd: *K1, sl2tog kw, K1, p2sso, rep from * around—34 (38) sts.

Next rnd: Knit.

Next rnd: *Sl2tog kw, K1, p2sso, K1, rep from * around to last 2 sts, end K2tog—17 (19) sts.

Next rnd: Knit.

Next rnd: *K1, sl2tog kw, K1, p2sso, rep from * around to last 1 (3) st, K1 (K1, K2tog)—9 (10) sts. Break yarn, thread through tapestry needle, and draw through rem sts. Weave in ends.

Booties Instructions

With A and size 6 dpns, CO 40 sts. Join into rnd, being careful not to twist sts, and PM.

Ruffle

Rnds 1–3: *P1, K3, rep from * around.

Rnd 4: *P1, sl2tog kw, K1, p2sso, rep from * around—20 sts.

Change to B and knit 1 rnd.

Begin Pattern

Rnds 1 and 3: With B, *sl1 pw, K1, YO, pass slipped st over K1 and YO, rep from * around. Break B at end of rnd 3.

Rnd 2: With B, knit.

Rnd 4: With A, knit.

Heel

K10, turn and purl across same 10 sts—these are heel sts. Place rem 10 sts on holder.

Knit 8 rows, ending with a WS row.

Turn Heel

Row 1: K5, K2tog, K1.

Row 2: K2, K2tog, K1.

Row 3: K3, K2tog, K1.

Row 4: K4, K2tog, K1—6 sts. Break yarn.

Gusset

Sl first 3 heel sts onto dpn. PM to mark beg of rnd and rejoin B. K3, PU 4 sts along selvage of heel flap, PM (this will be a "gusset marker"), SSK, K6, K2tog from holder, PM (another "gusset marker"), PU 4 sts along other heel flap selvage, knit last 3 heel sts—22 sts.

Shape Gusset

Next rnd: Purl to 2 sts before first gusset marker, P2tog. Knit to next gusset marker, P2tog, purl to end of rnd—20 sts.

Next rnd: Knit.

Rep these 2 rnds until 16 sts rem.

Foot

Rnd 1: P4, K8, P4.

Rnd 2: Knit.

Rep these 2 rnds until you've worked 6 rnds total.

Shape Toe

Next rnd: P2, P2tog, SSK, K4, K2tog, P2tog, P2—12 sts.

Next rnd: Knit.

Next rnd: P1, P2tog, SSK, K2, K2tog, P2tog, P1—8 sts.

Break yarn, thread through tapestry needle, and draw through rem sts. Weave in ends.

Dots and Ruffles

Incorporating a simple yet effective dot stitch pattern and a structured ruffle border, this set is simple yet striking. The borders require casting on a lot of stitches, so be prepared to count (and re-count) your stitches.

KNITTED

Finished Sizes

Blanket: 30" x 32"

Hat: Newborn (0–6 Months, 1 Year, 2 Years)
14½ (16, 17½, 19)" circumference

Socks: 0–6 Months

Blanket Materials

◆ Provence from Classic Elite (100% cotton; 100 g; 205 yds) in the following colors 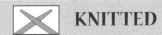 :

A	1 hank	2652 Purple
B	4 hanks	2649 Lilac

◆ Two 24" circular needles, both in size 5 (3.75 mm), or size required to obtain gauge

◆ 1 additional size 5 (3.75 mm) needle for attaching ruffles with 3-needle bind off; can be straight, circular, or double-pointed needle)

◆ Tapestry needle

Hat and Socks Materials

◆ Provence from Classic Elite (100% cotton; 100 g; 205 yds) in the following colors 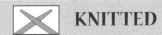 :

A	1 hank	2652 Purple
B	1 hank	2649 Lilac

◆ **For hat:** 16" circular needle in size 5 (3.75 mm), size 5 (3.75 mm) double-pointed needles

◆ **For socks:** Size 4 (3.5 mm) double-pointed needles, stitch holder, or waste yarn

◆ Stitch marker

◆ Tapestry needle

Gauge

21 sts and 30 rows = 4" in dot st patt on size 5 needle

Dot Stitch Pattern

(Odd-numbered rows are RS rows.)

Row 1: Knit.

Row 2 and all even-numbered rows: Purl.

Row 3: K2, *K3, P1, rep from * across, end K5.

Row 5: Knit.

Row 7: K3, *P1, K3, rep from * across, end P1, K3.

Ruffle

(Even-numbered rows are RS rows.)

Row 1: P7, *K1, P7, rep from * across.

Row 2: K2, sl2tog kw, K1, p2sso, K2, *P1, K2, sl2tog kw, K1, p2sso, K2, rep from * across.

Row 3: P5, *K1, P5, rep from * across.

Row 4: K1, sl2tog kw, K1, p2sso, K1, *P1, K1, sl2tog kw, K1, p2sso, K1, rep from * across.

Row 5: Knit.

Blanket Instructions

With A and 24" circular needle in size 5, CO 303 sts.

Work rows 1–5 of ruffle—151 sts. Break A.

Change to B and beg dot st patt. Work rows 1–8 for 28 times, and then work rows 1–4 one more time. Break B. Leave sts on needle and set aside.

Top Ruffle

With A and 24" circular needle in size 5, CO 303 sts.

Work rows 1–5 of ruffle—151 sts. Do not break A.

Join Top Ruffle to Blanket

With RS of top ruffle and blanket facing each other, and using A, join with 3-needle BO (see page 8).

Side Ruffles

With A and size 5 circular needle, CO 343 sts.

Work rows 1–5 of ruffle—171 sts. Do not break A.

With RS facing and B, PU 171 sts along side selvage. Break B. Using A, join side ruffle to blanket with 3-needle BO.

Work 2nd side ruffle the same way.

Block blanket so that ruffles lie flat (see page 12).

Hat Instructions

With 16" circular needle in size 5 and A, CO 152 (168, 184, 200) sts. Join into rnd, being careful not to twist sts, and PM.

Work ruffle as follows:

Rnd 1: *P1, K7, rep from * around.

Rnd 2: *P1, K2, sl2tog kw, K1, p2sso, K2, rep from * around.

Rnd 3: *P1, K5, rep from * around.

Rnd 4: *P1, K1, sl2tog kw, K1, p2sso, K1, rep from * around—76 (84, 92, 100) sts.

Rnd 5: Purl. Break A.

Change to B, knit 1 rnd, and then work twisted knitting patt as follows:

Rnds 1 and 3: *K1 tbl, rep from * around.

Rnds 2 and 4: *K1 tbl, sl1 pw, rep from * around.

After completing 4 rnds of twisted knitting, beg dot st patt as follows:

Rnds 1 and 2: Knit.

Rnd 3: *P1, K3, rep from * around.

Rnds 4, 5, and 6: Knit

Rnd 7: K2, P1, *K3, P1, rep from * around, end K1.

Rnd 8: Knit.

Work rnds 1–8 another 4 (4, 5, 5) times, and then work rnds 1–2 one more time.

Next rnd: *P1, sl2tog kw, K1, p2sso, rep from * around—38 (42, 46, 50) sts.

Next rnd: Knit.

Next rnd: *Sl2tog kw, K1, p2sso, K1, rep from * around to last 2 sts, end K2tog—19 (21, 23, 25) sts.

Next rnd: Knit.

Next rnd: *K1, sl2tog kw, K1, p2sso, rep from * around to last 3 (1, 3, 1) sts.

Sizes Newborn and 1 Year, end K1, K2tog—10 (12) sts.

Sizes 0–6 Months and 2 Years, end K1—11 (13) sts.

Break yarn, thread through tapestry needle, and draw through rem sts.

Socks Instructions

With A and size 4 dpn, CO 22 sts. Divide sts over 3 dpns, join in rnd, and PM.

Work K1, P1 ribbing for 2".

Knit 2 rnds, knitting 2tog at beg of second rnd—21 sts. Break A.

Heel

Join B and knit 1 rnd.

Next rnd: K10, turn and purl across same 10 sts—these are heel sts. Place rem 11 sts on holder or waste yarn.

Next row: Knit.

Next row: Purl.

Rep these 2 rows 2 more times.

Turn Heel

Row 1: K5, K2tog, K1.

Row 2: P2, P2tog tbl, P1.

Row 3: K3, K2tog, K1.

Row 4: P4, P2tog tbl, P1—6 sts.

Gusset

Sl first 3 heel sts onto dpn. PM to mark beg of rnd, K3, PU 5 sts along selvage of heel flap, PM (this will be a "gusset marker"), K11 sts from holder, PM (another "gusset marker"), PU 5 sts along other heel flap selvage, knit last 3 heel sts—27 sts.

Gusset and Foot

Rnd 1: Knit to 2 sts before first gusset marker, K2tog, knit to next gusset marker, SSK, knit to end of rnd—25 sts.

Rnd 2 and all alt rnds: Knit.

Rnd 3: Knit to 2 sts before first gusset marker, K2tog, K1, (P1, K3) 2 times, P1, K1, SSK, knit to end of rnd—23 sts.

Rnd 5: Knit to 2 sts before first gusset marker, K2tog, knit to next gusset marker, SSK, knit to end of rnd—21 sts.

Rnd 7: K5, (K3, P1) 2 times, K8.

Rnds 9 and 13: Knit

Rnd 11: K6, (P1, K3) 2 times, P1, K6.

Rnd 15: K5, (K3, P1) 2 times, K8.

Rnd 16: Knit.

Shape Toe

Next rnd: K3, K2tog, SSK, K7, K2tog, SSK, K3—17 sts.

Next rnd: Knit.

Next rnd: K2, K2tog, SSK, K2, P1, K2, K2tog, SSK, K2—13 sts.

Break yarn, thread through tapestry needle, and draw through rem sts. Weave in ends.

Pinwheel

Essentially a giant crochet square, the stitch variation in this blanket creates a pretty pinwheel shape. The light, airy fabric makes this a good option for a carry-along blanket. The lacy cap and booties make a pretty accompaniment to the blanket.

CROCHETED

Finished Sizes

Blanket: 31½" x 31½"

Cap: 0–6 Months

Booties: 0–6 Months

Blanket Materials

- Cotton Patine from Elsebeth Lavold (100% cotton; 50 g; 110 m) in the following colors **3** :

A	2 skeins	02 Alabaster
B	2 skeins	01 Porcelain
C	2 skeins	03 Driftwood
D	2 skeins	05 Damson

- Size 7 (4.5 mm) crochet hook
- Tapestry needle

Cap and Booties Materials

- Cotton Patine from Elsebeth Lavold (100% cotton; 50 g; 110 m) in the following colors **3** :

  Leftovers of yarns A and B from blanket

  1 additional skein of yarn C (03 Driftwood)

- Size 7 (4.5 mm) crochet hook
- Tapestry needle
- **For cap:** 1 yard of ⅝"-wide ribbon
- **For booties:** Size G-6 (4 mm) crochet hook, size 7 (4.5 mm) crochet hook, 1 yard of ¼"-wide ribbon

Gauge

11 sts and 8½ rnds = 4" in patt on size 7 crochet hook

NOTE: The gauge will get looser with each subsequent round as the blanket gets bigger. Gauge given above is an average.

Blanket Instructions

Rnd 1: With A, ch 4, join last ch to first ch with sl st to form a ring.

Rnd 2: With A, ch 3 (counts as 1 dc), 2 dc in ring, (ch 1, 3 dc in ring) 3 times, ch 1, join with sl st in top of starting ch 3. Break A.

Rnd 3: With RS facing, join B in any ch-1 sp. Ch 3 (counts as 1 dc), 4 dc in same sp for corner, 1 dc between 2nd and 3rd st of next 3 dc group, (5 dc in next ch-1 sp, 1 dc between 2nd and 3rd st of next 3 dc group) 3 times, join last st of rnd to top of starting ch 3 with sl st. Break B.

Rnd 4: With RS facing, join C between 3rd and 4th sts of any corner group. Ch 3 (counts as 1 dc), 5 dc in same sp for corner, (3 dc in next single dc, 6 dc between 3rd and 4th sts of next corner group) 3 times, 3 dc in next single dc, join last st of rnd to top of starting ch 3 with sl st. Break C.

Rnd 5: With RS facing, join D between third and fourth sts of any corner group. Ch 3 (counts as 1 dc), 5 dc in same sp, 3 dc between fifth and sixth sts of same corner group, (3 dc between second and third sts of next 3 dc group, 3 dc between first and second sts of next corner group, 6 dc between third and fourth sts of same corner group, 3 dc between fifth and sixth sts of same corner group) 3 times, 3 dc between second and third sts of next 3 dc group, 3 dc between first and second sts of next corner group, join last st of rnd to starting ch 3 with sl st. Break D.

Rnd 6: With RS facing, join A between third and fourth sts of any corner group. Ch 3 (counts as 1 dc), 5 dc in same sp, 3 dc between fifth and sixth sts of same corner group, (3 dc between second and third sts of each of the next 3 dc groups, 3 dc between first and second sts of next corner group, 6 dc between third and fourth sts of same corner group, 3 dc between fifth and sixth sts of same corner group) 3 times, 3 dc between second and third sts of each of next 3 dc groups, 3 dc between first and second sts of next corner group, join last st of rnd to starting ch 3 with sl st. Break A.

Rnd 7: Work as rnd 6 with C.

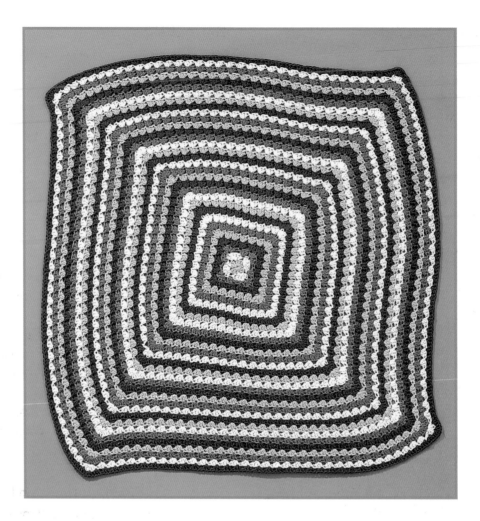

Rnd 8: Work as rnd 6 with B.

Rnd 9: Work as rnd 6 with D.

Rnd 10 (note that in this rnd you will not be inc so you will not add 3 dc to either side of corner 6 dc group): With RS facing, join A between 3rd and 4th sts of any corner group. Ch 3 (counts as 1 dc), 5 dc in same sp, (3 dc between 2nd and 3rd sts of each 3 dc group across to corner, 6 dc between 3rd and 4th sts of corner group) 3 times, 3 dc between 2nd and 3rd sts of each 3 dc group across, join last st of rnd to starting ch 3 with sl st. Break A.

Rnd 11 (inc rnd): With RS facing, join B between third and fourth sts of any corner group. Ch 3 (counts as 1 dc), 5 dc in same sp, 3 dc between fifth and sixth sts of same corner group, (3 dc between second and third sts of each 3 dc group across, 3 dc between first and second sts of next corner group, 6 dc between third and fourth sts of same corner group, 3 dc between fifth and sixth sts of same corner group) 3 times, 3 dc between

second and third sts of each 3 dc group across, 3 dc between first and second sts of next corner group, join last st of rnd to starting ch 3 with sl st. Break B.

Rnd 12: Work as rnd 10 with C.

Rnd 13: Work as rnd 11 with D.

Rnd 14: Work as rnd 10 with A.

Rnd 15: Work as rnd 11 with C.

Rnd 16: Work as rnd 10 with B.

Rnd 17: Work as rnd 11 with D.

Rnd 18: Work as rnd 10 with A.

Rnd 19: Work as rnd 11 with B.

Rnd 20: Work as rnd 10 with C.

Rnd 21: Work as rnd 11 with D.

Rnd 22: Work as rnd 10 with A.

Rnd 23: Work as rnd 11 with C.

Rnd 24: Work as rnd 10 with B.

Rnd 25: Work as rnd 11 with D.

Rnd 26: Work as rnd 10 with A.

Rnd 27: Work as rnd 11 with B.

Rnd 28: Work as rnd 10 with C.

Rnd 29: Work as rnd 11 with D.

Rnd 30: Work as rnd 10 with A.

Rnd 31: Work as rnd 11 with C.

Rnd 32: Work as rnd 10 with B.

Rnd 33: Work as rnd 11 with D.

Break D and fasten off. Weave in ends. Gently block blanket into shape.

Enlarging the Blanket

To make the blanket larger, simply continue pattern as established, alternating round 10 and round 11, until it's the size you want, ending with round 11 completed.

Cap Instructions

Back

With A, ch 4, join last ch to first ch with sl st to form a ring.

Rnd 1 (RS): With A, ch 3 (counts as 1 dc), 2 dc in ring, (ch 1, 3 dc in ring) 3 times, ch 1, join with sl st in top of starting ch 3. Break A.

Rnd 2: With RS facing, join B in any ch-1 sp. Ch 3 (counts as 1 dc), 4 dc in same sp for corner, 1 dc between 2nd and 3rd sts of next 3 dc group, (5 dc in next ch-1 sp, 1 dc between 2nd and 3rd sts of next 3 dc group) 3 times, join last st of rnd to top of starting ch 3 with sl st. Break B.

Rnd 3: With RS facing, join C between 3rd and 4th sts of any corner group, ch 3, 2 dc in same st, (sk next st, 3 dc in next st) 11 times, sk last st, sl st in top of beg ch—36 sts.

Rnd 4: Ch 3, 2 dc in sl st sp (base of ch), sk next st, 3 dc in next st, sk next st, 2 dc in next st, *(sk next st, 3 dc in next st) twice, sk next st, 2 dc in next st, rep from * around, sk last st, sl st in top of beg ch—48 sts.

Rnd 5: Ch 3, 2 dc in sl st sp (base of ch), sk next st, 3 dc in next st, (sk next st, 2 dc in next st) twice, *(sk next st, 3 dc in next st) twice, (sk next st, 2 dc in next st) twice, rep from * around, end sk next st, sl st in top of beg ch—60 sts.

Top and Sides

Next row: Ch 3, dc at base of ch, (sk next st, 2 dc in next st) 23 times. Turn.

Next row: Ch 3, *2 dc in next st, sk next st, rep from * across, dc in top of tch.

Rep last row 5 more times. Break yarn and fasten off. Weave in ends.

Thread ribbon through front edge of cap.

Booties Instructions

With A and G-6 hook, ch 4, join last ch to first ch with sl st to form a ring.

Rnd 1: Ch 3 (counts as 1 dc), 2 dc in ring, (ch 1, 3 dc in ring) 3 times, ch 1, join with sl st in top of starting ch 3.

Rnd 2: Ch 3, dc in sl st sp (base of ch), sk next dc, 2 dc in next dc, *sk next ch, 2 dc in next dc, sk next dc, 2 dc in next dc, rep from * around, sl st in top of beg ch—16 dc.

Rows 3 and 4: Ch 3, dc in first dc, *sk next dc, 2 dc in next dc, rep from * around, sl st in top of beg ch.

Heel

Change to size 7 hook, ch 1 and sc in first 6 dc. Turn.

(Ch 1, sc in next 12 sts, turn) for 2 rows.

Ch 1, sc in next 4 sts, (sc2tog) twice, sc in next 4 sts, turn—10 sts.

Ch 1, sc across row, turn.

Ch 1, sc in next 3 sts, (sc2tog) twice, sc in next 3 sts, turn—8 sts.

Ch 1, sc across row. Break yarn and fasten off.

Sew heel seam.

With size 7 hook, join A at back of heel and work sc 2 rnds around foot opening. Break yarn and fasten off. Weave in ends.

Thread ribbon around foot opening.

Tip

A pair of thin socks worn underneath will keep Baby's toes from poking through the open fabric of the bootie.

No Gauge

Knit diagonally from corner to corner, this is a blanket you can make in any size you want, and with whatever yarn you want. The pattern is reversible and can be used as a ground for appliqué, embroidery, or other embellishments. The hat is worked from the top down, allowing you to size as you go. And the socks are simply a spiral that conforms to a baby's foot. They're admittedly a little funny looking, but they're also fast and easy, and they stay on as well as the fanciest booties!

KNITTED

Finished Sizes

Blanket: 22" x 22"

Hat: Newborn (0–6 Months, 6–18 Months)
14½ (16, 17½)" circumference

Socks: 0–6 Months

Blanket Materials

- Cotton Fleece from Brown Sheep Company (80% cotton, 20% merino wool; 3.5 oz; 215 yds) in the following colors 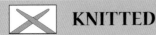 :
  2 skeins of CW150 Antique Lace

  Small amounts of additional colors for floral appliqué. Colors shown in sample are CW105 Putty, CW832 Silver Plum, and CW715 Plum Patina.

- 24" circular needle in size 6 (4 mm)
- Tapestry needle

NOTE: The blanket needs to be blocked into shape when completed, so it is best worked in natural fiber yarns. If you are unsure if your yarn will block, experiment with a small test swatch.

Hat Materials

- Cotton Fleece from Brown Sheep Company (80% cotton, 20% merino wool; 3.5 oz; 215 yds) in the following colors 4 :
  1 skein   CW-715 Plum Patina

  Optional: Small amount of yarn in contrasting color for floral appliqué

- Split-ring stitch marker
- Tapestry needle
- **Newborn only:** Size 6 (4 mm) double-pointed needles, size 5 (3.75 mm) double-pointed needles
- **All other sizes:** Size 6 (4 mm) double-pointed needles, 16" circular needle in size 6 (4 mm), 16" circular needle in size 5 (3.75 mm)

Socks Materials

- Small amount of leftover yarn from blanket or hat
- Size 6 (4 mm) double-pointed needles

- Split-ring stitch marker
- Tapestry needle

Gauge

Blanket as shown:

18 sts and 31 rows = 4" in patt on size 6 needle

20 sts and 28 rows = 4" in St st on size 6 needle

Blanket Instructions

CO 3 sts.

Set-up rows:

Row 1 (WS): (K1f&b) 2 times, K1—5 sts.

Rows 2 and 4: Knit.

Row 3: K1f&b, K1, P1, K1f&b, K1.

Pattern

Row 1 (WS): K1f&b,*K1, P1, rep from * to last 2 sts, K1f&b, K1—9 sts.

Row 2: Knit.

Rep these 2 rows until selvage length equals desired blanket width or you've used up half your yarn, ending with row 2.

Begin Decreasing

Row 1: K1, K2tog, *K1, P1, rep from * to last 4 sts, K1, SSK, K1.

Row 2: Knit.

Rep these 2 rows until 7 sts rem, ending with row 2.

Final Decreases

Row 1: K1, K2tog, K1, SSK, K1—5 sts.

Row 2 (BO row): K1, K3tog, K1, BO as you go.

Block blanket into shape. The completed blanket will be in the shape of an elongated diamond and needs to be shaped into a square. This is best accomplished by wet blocking (see page 12).

Design Option

Apply floral appliqués, or embroider a monogram or other design as desired.

Hat Instructions

With size 6 dpn, CO 4 sts.

K1f&b into each st—8 sts.

Divide onto 4 dpns, placing 2 sts on each needle. Join into rnd, PM in first st of rnd.

Placing Markers

When working with a small number of stitches on double-pointed needles, the markers that sit on the needle have a tendency to slip off. I prefer to place a marker in the stitch itself. You'll need a split-ring marker (or a paper clip if you are in a pinch) to do this. Just remember to replace the marker into the first stitch of each subsequent round.

Knit 1 rnd.

Next rnd: K1f&b in each st—16 sts.

Next rnd: Knit.

Next rnd: *K1f&b, K1, rep from * around—24 sts.

Next rnd: Knit.

Next rnd: *K1f&b, K2, rep from * around—32 sts.

Next rnd: Knit.

Next rnd: *K1f&b, K3, rep from * around—40 sts.

Next rnd: Knit.

Next rnd: *K1f&b, K4, rep from * around—48 sts.

Next rnd: Knit.

Next rnd: *K1f&b, K5, rep from * around—56 sts.

Next rnd: Knit.

Cont in this manner, inc 8 sts every other rnd as established, until you reach the circumference you want (divide desired circumference by st gauge to determine the number of sts you need, and then rnd off to the closest multiple of 8).

For sizes as given, inc until you have 72 (80, 88) sts, changing to 16" circular needle when possible.

Cont to knit in rnds without inc until hat measures 4½ (5, 5½)" from top of crown.

Change to size 5 dpn or 16" size 5 circular needle and beg band.

Flower

With size 6 dpn, CO 49 sts.

Row 1: P6, *K1, P5, rep from *, end K1, P6.

Row 2: K2, *sl2tog kw, K1, psso, K1, P1, K1, rep from *, end sl2tog kw, K1, psso, K2—33 sts.

Rows 3 and 5: Knit the knits and purl the purls.

Row 4: K1, *sl2tog kw, K1, psso, P1, rep from *, end sl2tog kw, K1, psso, K1—17 sts.

Break yarn, leaving a 6" tail. With tapestry needle, thread yarn through loops on knitting needle and gather knitting into a circle. Seam edges. Work in ends.

Leaf

With size 6 dpn, CO 13 sts.

Row 1: P6, K1, P6.

Rep rows 2–5 of flower.

Break yarn, leaving a 6" tail. With tapestry needle, thread yarn through loops on knitting needle and gather knitting into a wedge. Work in ends.

Make as many flowers and leaves as you wish. Sew into place. Add French knots (see page 12) in the center of the flowers.

Band

Rnd 1: *K1, P1, rep from * around.

Rnds 2 and 4: Knit.

Rnd 3: *P1, K1, rep from * around.

Work rnds 1–4 one time, and then rnd 1 one more time.

Knit 4 rnds.

BO in K1, P1. Weave in ends.

Making Matching Sets

You can easily make a matching parent-child set of hats using this top down design. For an adult size, simply continue to increase as established until the hat fits an adult head (sample shown was increased to 104 stitches), and then work even until hat is 1½" short of desired crown height, change to smaller size needle, and work band as for baby hat.

Socks Instructions

These socks are started at the toe, increased to the circumference of a baby's foot, and then worked in a spiraling K2, P2 rib that makes them conform to a baby's foot and leg.

With size 6 dpn, CO 4 sts.

K1f&b into each st—8 sts.

Divide onto 4 dpns, placing 2 sts on each needle. Join into the rnd, placing a marker in the first st of the rnd.

Knit 1 rnd.

Next rnd: K1f&b in each st—16 sts.

Next rnd: Knit.

(For bulkier yarns, this may be all the increases you need and you can proceed to spiral rib.)

Next rnd: *K1f&b, K3, rep from * around—20 sts.

Next rnd: Knit.

If you need to make the sock bigger, rep the above 2 rnds, working 1 more st after each inc, until the sock is the size you want, and then proceed to spiral rib. For the sock shown here, I increased to 20 sts only. For socks worked in finer yarns or in larger sizes, you may need to inc to 24 or even 28 sts before starting the ribbing.

Spiral Rib

Rnds 1–4: *K2, P2, rep from * around.

Rnds 5–8: P1, *K2, P2, rep from * around to last 3 sts, end K2, P1.

Rnds 9–12: *P2, K2, rep from * around.

Rnds 14–16: K1, *P2, K2, rep from * around to last 3 sts, end P2, K1.

Cont as established, shifting the ribbing 1 st to the left every 4 rnds, until sock is the length you want. I think 4" is a good length for sizes Newborn to 0–6 Months; it gives you enough length to fold down the top for a cuff if you like.

BO in patt. Weave in ends.

Ensuring a Good Fit

You need a relaxed bind off to ensure that the socks will fit over a baby's foot. If you tend to bind off tightly, work the last couple of rounds on double-pointed needles one size larger than those used for the rest of the sock, binding off with these larger needles as well.

Alphabet

Here is a basic alphabet that can be used to personalize your knit and crochet projects. The letters can be added using duplicate stitch embroidery, cross stitch, or with 2-color techniques. I find that letters added by embossing (purling the letters on a stockinette stitch ground) often need to be quite a bit larger to really show up, so if you wish to add letters with embossing you probably need to find or design a larger alphabet.

The best source I have found for alphabets is cross-stitch sampler books. A quick trip to your local bookstore or library should turn up a variety of references and a multitude of alphabets. In the meantime, the alphabet here can get you started. The letters and numbers are based on an eighteenth-century Quaker sampler.

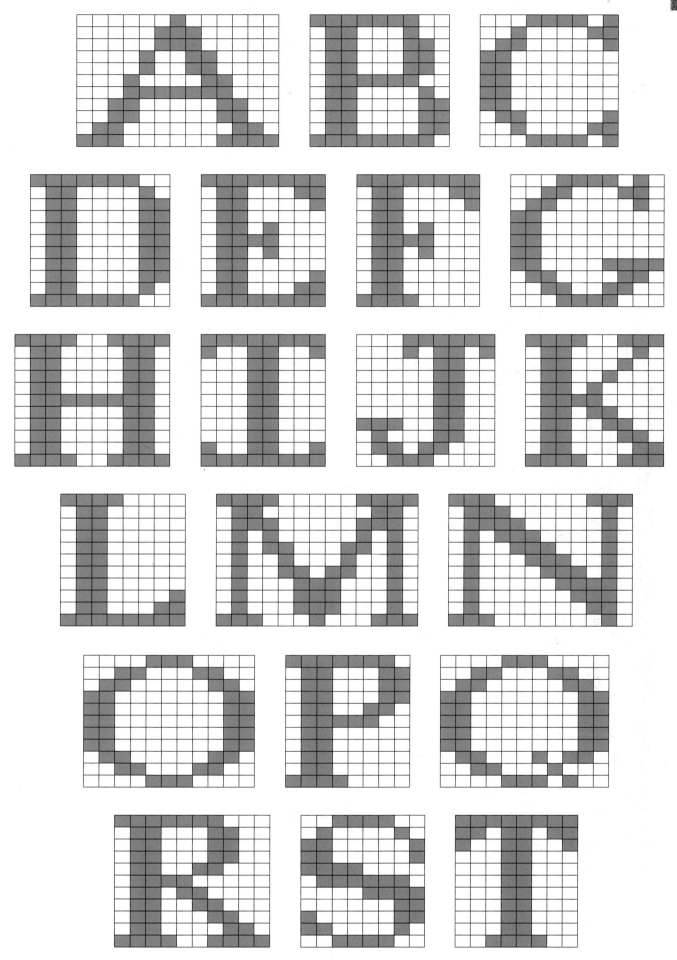